METHOD
IN THE
MADNESS

Praise for the Book

'Param has worn more professional hats through his forty-year-long career than anyone I can think of! The Insider-Outsider-Insider captures his fascinating journey and leaves the reader with simple yet powerful insights on how to approach life and work with a can-do attitude. These are lessons in management that one can't learn at business school. A must-read!'

—*Nandan Nilekani*
Chairman and Co-Founder of Infosys and Founding Chairman of UIDAI (Aadhaar)

'Parameswaran Iyer's *Method in the Madness* is the riveting story of a can-do IAS officer with a front-row seat to history. He fought illegal miners, saved Sikh families in 1984, worked with the Defence Minister during the Bofors years, caught man-eating tigers and went on to become a travelling evangelist for toilet use, implementing the world's largest behaviour change programme. Iyer also peppers the book with pro-tips, and advocates a system that offers young IAS officers an area of specialization for their work.'

—*Shekhar Gupta*
Founder and Editor-in-chief, The Print

'In the management literature on decisions we have conventionally focused on description-based decisions where risky prospects involving the chance of possible outcomes are described such as in drug package inserts and mutual fund brochures. In much of life, unfortunately, we have to face decisions where we do not have explicit descriptions of possible outcomes such as of an accident on crossing a busy street or achieving desirable outcomes on taking up a job and such experience-based decisions are not adequately studied in management literature. This book tells us that in experience-based decisions low-probability events are given low weight – such as the chance of making it through the civil services or of an injury impeding a promising sports career or making India open-defecation free – and that provides insights about choices that we all would gain from since formal education or training would never expose us to such frames of mind by which to steer through life.'

—*Prof. Errol D'Souza*
Director, IIM Ahmedabad

'*Method in the Madness* is a rattling good read, full of twists and turns, setbacks and triumphs, peppered with pro-tips for life and work. Param's unconventional approach to disruption at the workplace is exactly what is needed to make a success of large-scale transformative projects.'

—*Dr Valerie Curtis*
Professor, London School of Hygiene and Tropical Medicine

'*Method in the Madness* is as unique a book as has been the career of Param Iyer. Written with humour and wisdom, this professional memoir gives rare insight into what it takes to succeed, regardless of where one is in their career. From cracking the IAS to leaving it to being the frontman of India's sanitation revolution, Param has been the CEO of his career and, in this valuable chronicle, he is redefining the rules of business and what it truly means to be a civil servant.'

—*Amitabh Kant*
CEO, NITI Aayog

'Successful bureaucrats aren't supposed to be "Insider-Outsiders". Yet Param Iyer offers an absorbing account of his own such personal journey – traversing the IAS and the World Bank, being a full-time parent–tennis coach, and finally spearheading the implementation of the Swachh Bharat programme. In doing so he offers real-life, from-the-heart management lessons that you won't find in a business school curriculum.'

—*Bharat Anand*
Henry R. Byers Professor of Business Administration, Harvard Business School, and author of The Content Trap

'Param Iyer will always be associated with India's most audacious public health venture, the Swachh Bharat Mission. His account of the country's sanitation transformation and its impact on age-old beliefs and habits is an outstanding window into the world of governance and management – and a blueprint for creating a social revolution. An inspirational and impactful story.'

—*Mark Suzman*
CEO, Bill & Melinda Gates Foundation

'It is not often that you come across a book that makes you laugh, think and learn, all at the same time. Param Iyer's *Method in the Madness* is one such rare book. He takes the reader on a journey spanning decades and continents. The anecdotes from his life range from the hilarious to the sombre to the exciting, with never a dull moment. Young readers would do well to take notes as he generously shares his unique professional trajectory and vital career lessons. A fun yet educational read, packed full with pro-tips and insights, this book is a must-read for those who believe that working together can achieve social progress.'

—*Naina Lal Kidwai*
Founder Chair, India Sanitation Coalition
Chair, FICCI Water Mission, and past president, FICCI

'Param's unconventional career makes for fascinating reading, particularly his mid-career break to become a coach to a professional tennis player, his daughter, Tara, who was one of India's top tennis players. His is a great example of how learnings from sport can be successfully applied to any man–management setting. Very insightful.'

—*Vijay Amritraj*
Former tennis player and sports commentator

'Param Iyer combines the art of simple storytelling with a set of practical management insights for all readers, from business school students to young, or even more seasoned, professionals. The book is a peek into an extraordinary life, combining a career in public service with raising a sports-mad family, as Param moves from small-town Uttar Pradesh to Washington DC, Egypt, Lebanon, Hanoi and back to India. His sense of purpose and the unique experiences he gained transforming India's sanitation landscape provide the backdrop to his "pro-tips", simple lessons that contribute to getting an impossible job done. Throughout, Param's humour and optimism shine through, and are amongst the most important lessons to take away from this engaging book.'

—*Anu Madgavkar*
Partner, McKinsey Global Institute

'Parameswaran Iyer has had an inspiring, amazing life, and the Swachh Bharat Mission, which he implemented, has achieved an extraordinary amount in terms of health, safety, and even gender equality. It is a superb and practical example of the "nudge approach" at scale. For managers everywhere, this brilliant, astonishing book is must reading.'

—*Cass R. Sunstein*
Robert Walmsley University Professor, Harvard University,
and co-author, Nudge

METHOD
IN THE
MADNESS

*Insights from My Career as an
Insider-Outsider-Insider*

PARAMESWARAN IYER

HarperCollins *Publishers* India

First published in India by
HarperCollins *Publishers* in 2021
A-75, Sector 57, Noida, Uttar Pradesh 201301, India
www.harpercollins.co.in

2 4 6 8 10 9 7 5 3 1

Copyright © Parameswaran Iyer 2021

Inside illustrations by Ishan Trivedi

P-ISBN: 978-93-9032-756-0
E-ISBN: 978-93-9032-757-7

Typeset in 11/15.2 Sabon LT Std at
Manipal Technologies Limited, Manipal

Printed and bound at
Replika Press Pvt. Ltd.

This book is produced from independently certified FSC® paper to
ensure responsible forest management.

For Indira, Tara and Venkat

Contents

Acknowledgements

THERE ARE MANY people I would like to thank for participating in my journey.

My family – my wife and anchor, Indira, for her unstinting support, out-of-the box ideas and balancing the dual responsibility of steadying the family ship and a career, allowing me the flexibility to go inside–outside–inside. She also played a key role in advising on the theme, tone and contents of this book. And our daughter and son – Tara and Venkat – for their backing all along, indulgently allowing their dad to fulfil his road manager aspirations, and for pleasantly surprising me by actually going through the manuscript – and telling me bluntly what they liked and what they didn't!

My parents – my late mother, Kalyani, for her dedication to the family and instilling core values in her three children, and my father, the 'running' Air Marshal, to whom I owe so much, and who continues to inspire me and countless others in so many ways. And my two sisters, Mina and Indu, who have steadfastly supported me in all my endeavours from childhood onwards.

My colleagues in the IAS – especially my seniors, who mentored me along the way. A special mention needs to be made of two former Cabinet Secretaries – Kamal Pande and P.K. Sinha, for their guidance over the years. I would also like to thank Rajiv Mehrishi and Amitabh Kant for their friendship and counsel during my term as Secretary to the Government of India.

Team Swachh Bharat Mission – whose wholehearted effort and 'can do' spirit made achievement of the goal possible. In particular, Arun Baroka, Akshay Rout, V. Radha, Samir Kumar, Yugal Joshi, Seemantinee Sengupta, O.P. Agarwal, Anand Shekhar, Sharad Kumar, and many others. My thanks are also due to the state SBM teams – Principal Secretaries, Mission Directors, State Coordinators; the District teams – led by the incomparable District Magistrates, District Coordinators, the Zila Swachh Bharat Preraks; and last but certainly not least – the Sarpanches and the thousands and thousands of our grassroots-level storm troopers, the swachhagrahis.

My office team – Surendra Gosain and my three executive assistants: Mahima Vashisht, Vineet Jain and Karishma Kadyan. Apart from the energy and enthusiasm the three brought to the job, they were of great help in extensively reviewing the manuscript.

The late Professor Val Curtis of the London School of Hygiene and Tropical Medicine for her friendship, collaboration and guidance over the years, as well as for her valuable comments on the manuscript.

The HarperCollins team, Krishan Chopra and Siddhesh Inamdar, for their guidance and assistance.

Finally, and crucially, I owe my second insider stint to Prime Minister Narendra Modi. He gave me the incredible, life-changing opportunity to serve my country, for which I will always be grateful.

Introduction

AT THE OUTSET, let me reassure any intrepid reader who has taken the risk of opening this book that this is not just another memoir of a retired civil servant being inflicted upon an unsuspecting public.

Why not? Well, because my career, as the title of the book suggests, has indeed been rather unconventional. In fact, you may want to fasten your seatbelt as you continue reading because the following merry-go-round description is bound to leave you a little dizzy!

I was an Indian Administrative Service (IAS) officer for about seventeen years, then took leave of absence from the IAS and joined the World Bank in Washington DC. I resigned from the World Bank after six years to become a road manager to a professional tennis player, who happened to be my daughter. Two years later, I returned to the IAS, then quit permanently a year later to rejoin the World Bank. Six years later I left the World Bank again, this time to join as one of the longest-serving Secretaries to the Government of India, managing the Swachh

Bharat Mission. In government-speak, or *sarkari* jargon, I have
been a rather unique Insider–Outsider–Insider.

One consistent thread throughout my journey, though,
has been the 'madness' I have faced along the way. The term
'madness' for me symbolizes the many different aspects of our
work and lives that we face over the course of our careers – the
pressure, the tough deadlines, the politics, the camaraderie,
the chaos, the fun, the highs and lows and, above all, the
unpredictability. I tried to bring some method to the madness
and hence the title of the book, courtesy of my wife, Indira.

As you go through this book, you will traverse the journey
of my four-decade-long career, packaged in three sections and
sixteen chapters. The title of every chapter reflects a key insight
acquired along the way. You will also find some practical 'pro-
tips' sprinkled throughout the book – tips that they usually don't
teach in business schools or in civil service academies, but which
I believe are crucial to succeed in one's career.

I have also resisted the urge to recount my entire life history by
restricting this tale to only my career years. You will find none of
the 'I was born in Srinagar in 1959' stuff in this book. The first
twenty years of my life have been chopped out; my story begins
in the year 1979, just after I returned from the US, having spent
a year studying there. It ends, in the book, in August 2020, after
I finished my tenure as Secretary to the Government of India.

In writing this book, I have tried to bring out the relentless
curiosity, love of a challenge and the drive to find practical
solutions to problems – all of which have motivated me for forty
years. It has been an incredible journey, and I hope it will be a
fun and useful trip for you too.

INSIDER (1979–1998)

3 September 1979

JFK ✈ DEL
AI 112

I WAS AT JFK airport in New York, checking in for Air India's flight to Delhi via London. I had just completed a year on an exchange scholarship at Davidson College, North Carolina, and a two-month stint teaching tennis at Nick Bollettieri's summer tennis camp for children at Beaver Dam, Wisconsin, to earn some money. Fully equipped with six 'Red Heads' – aluminium-framed tennis rackets that were the rage those days, I was young and excited about returning to my country to try out a tennis career.

When the Air India agent asked me to include these precious tennis rackets with my checked-in baggage, I protested. 'The tennis rackets are fragile and may get damaged if kept in the hold. Besides, my profession depends on them.' When the agent raised her eyebrows, I quickly fibbed, 'As you know, the US Open tennis championships are currently going on – I'm a professional tennis player and having just lost in the qualifying rounds of the tournament, I'm returning to India to resume playing on the national tennis circuit. You would really be doing me a huge favour by allowing me to carry my rackets on board with me,' and flashed a smile with as much charisma as I could muster.

The agent gave me a sceptical look but allowed me to take my rackets on board as carry-on luggage. I felt justified in uttering the half-truth, since I actually planned to give the professional tennis tour a shot on returning to India.

Unable to stretch out much on the long flight back, I was a little stiff when we landed in Delhi the next day. It felt great to be back and I received a very warm welcome at the airport from my parents, Venky and Kalyani, and my two sisters, Mina and Indu. I had enjoyed my student year in the US but it was now time to think about making a living.

1

If you never try, you'll never know

EXPERIMENTS WITH TENNIS, HOTELS AND JOURNALISM — TO
FINALLY CRACKING THE IAS

WHILE SOME YOUNGSTERS are very clear about the kind of careers they want for themselves, there are others who are less certain. I fit into the latter category. Newly returned from the US after a year's study at Davidson College, North Carolina, I was 20 years old, gloriously unemployed and looked quite unemployable too. I was also not too sure what exactly I wanted to do with my life and decided to take my chances with different job opportunities, earnestly hoping that that one of them would eventually click, and maybe even lead me to my 'dream job'.

Trying for a sports career

Having earlier played on the St. Stephen's College and Delhi University tennis teams, and then in a few minor league tennis tournaments in the US, I was keen to try out as a professional tennis player on returning to India. The full support of my parents, Venky and Kalyani, the latter a tennis champion in her Queen Mary's College days in Madras (now Chennai), strengthened my resolve to attempt to make a living out of playing tennis.

As you may have guessed, my stint as a professional tennis player was brief and unsuccessful. Between October 1979 and early 1980, I played in Delhi, Chandigarh, Allahabad, Calcutta (now Kolkata) and Ahmedabad, and lost in the early rounds of all the tournaments. In Delhi, at the tennis nationals played on the Gymkhana Club grass courts, I lost convincingly to Davis Cupper Shyam Minotra in the first round. In January 1980, returning from Ahmedabad to Delhi by train in a three-tier compartment, I pondered over my future. The tennis career was evidently not working out but entering the conventional job market was not going to be easy. With only a bachelor's degree in English literature, albeit from a fancy college, and with stiff competition from all the engineering and medical students, my career prospects looked rather dim.

On my return to Delhi, there was a family council to discuss what I should do next. My father, then a serving Group Captain in the Indian Air Force, felt that if I did not want to pursue a tennis career, I should consider doing a master's in English literature or study for a law degree. Mina, my eldest sister, later a lawyer, and Indu, my elder sister, a Russian language expert, were both keen tennis players themselves, with the latter having won many tournaments, and thought I should continue playing on the tennis circuit. My mother, always the realist, believed it was time for me to consider applying for a 'regular' job. Given all the conflicting suggestions, I decided to follow my mother's advice.

Attempting to take on market forces

I put my tennis career on hold and made a foray into the private sector job market. I first applied for a management trainee position at the Delhi Cloth Mills (DCM) company in Delhi and, to my surprise, was invited for an interview. The interview panel chairman was the venerable Dr Bharat Ram, the iconic industrialist who had built up the DCM corporate empire from scratch. After a few preliminary inquiries about my background and interest in the job, Dr Ram gently posed the killer question: 'Mr Iyer, do you know what "deflation" means?' Since my general knowledge at that time was limited to the sports news, I was stumped by this, and could only manage an embarrassed smile and a shake of the head. Dr Ram laughed and said: 'Young man, isn't it obvious – deflation is the opposite of inflation!' It wasn't all that obvious to me though, but what *was* very clear was that I wasn't getting the job. My next attempt, the same month, was to apply for a job – that of a 'Personnel Pupil' – at another fabled private company, the Indian Tobacco Company (ITC) in Calcutta. I took a train to Calcutta for the interview, and this time I thought it went off well but, needless to say, the result was the same – I flunked out. As consolation, I visited the famous Flury's bakery on Park Street for a delicious selection of biscuits and cakes to take home to Delhi.

Giving the holy grail – the civil services – a shot

Back in Delhi, my father, ever the optimist, brought up for the first time the idea of my taking the civil services examination. He had seen the Union Public Service Commission's (UPSC) recent full-page advertisement in the *Indian Express* and, half-seriously, suggested that I appear for the examination. 'You qualify to appear for the civil services examination with your bachelor's degree – why don't you give it a shot?' he said. I glanced at the advertisement and told my father that there was not much point in doing this, since the subject of my bachelor's degree, English literature, did not figure in the list of subjects that could be chosen for the preliminary exam. It turned out that the pattern of the civil services exam had changed just the previous year. From having just one written exam, the system had changed to a two-phase process, with a preliminary exam of objective-type questions and, for those who made it to the next round, a more traditional written exam with essay-type questions. My father suggested that we search for another subject I could take up for the preliminary examination. He went through the list of subjects with a fine-tooth comb and, finally, declared that my best bet for the preliminary exam was philosophy, since it appeared to have the shortest syllabus!

And so, I enlisted for the 1980 civil services preliminary exam, opting for philosophy as my subject. The other mandatory topic was general studies. With my limited general knowledge and my practically non-existent understanding of philosophy, I was quite certain that my foray into the civil services arena would be a colossal failure. My father, however, had other ideas. In those days, there were no *kunji*s (examination-focused guidebooks on specific topics). Besides, no one had heard of a subject like philosophy being assessed through 'objective-type' questions in the preliminary exam, a 100-item multiple choice test. Having to 'tick' the correct box out of a possible four answers – for philosophy – seemed a little crazy to me. Not quite knowing how to set about preparing for it, I struggled to find the appropriate textbooks to study from. Luckily, my father had a clear plan. Based then at the Air Force Station, Chakeri, Kanpur, he persuaded a professor at Kanpur University to prepare a sample objective-type question paper for me to try my hand at. Within a week I was presented with a paper featuring 100 questions, where all I had to do was tick one of the four options for each question and test my readiness to take the exam.

Prior to taking this mock test, I had done some cursory background reading on philosophy. So when I sat down to take the test, I hoped to do reasonably well. But it was not to be. Suffice it to say that I got only 10 answers correct out of 100. This was a bad start and confirmed my worst fears of failing the preliminary exam. The only silver lining was that the syllabus for the preliminary exam included a section on logic which interested me more than deep thinkers like Immanuel Kant, Ramanuja and Plato. Not that I was a whiz at logical thinking but at least it made more sense to me than the 'deeper' themes. To strengthen my logical thinking, I put in a burst of practice at answering questions like: 'If A hates B and B hates C, does A hate C?' While I wasn't too sure what the right answer to the question was, one thing I *was* sure about: I did not at all fancy my chances of clearing the preliminary exams.

From the sports page to the front page

To prepare for the general studies paper in the preliminary exam, I had no option but to read a couple of newspapers a day (the *Indian Express* and the *Times of India*) and, while my natural inclination was to go straight to the last (sports) page, I forced myself to read the front page headlines first to study the general and political news, followed by the pages with the economic and financial news and only then go to the sports page. As I went through this process, I have to admit that, despite myself, I gradually became interested in the broader news of the day rather than just which tennis player was the favourite to win Wimbledon that year. This budding curiosity about the world around me eventually developed into a deep interest and greatly strengthened my general knowledge and awareness, something which has stood me in good stead all through my career and life.

Finally, one hot summer day in May 1980, I took the Gomti Express train from Kanpur to Delhi to take the preliminary civil services exam at a government school in R.K. Puram. With very low expectations, I answered the two papers of the preliminary exam with panache, ticking one of the four options (A, B, C or D) for all the 100 questions in each paper, whether I knew the correct answer or not. Quite assured of not qualifying for the main examination, I nonchalantly returned to Kanpur, prepared to soon resume the hunt for an alternative career to the civil service.

To my disbelief, a couple of months later, I found I had qualified for the main exam after all. I could only surmise that my newly strengthened general awareness preparation had worked and I had probably also been more 'logical' than I thought in answering the logic questions; plus my tactic of consistently ticking option C for each question I was unsure about might have paid off (unlike today, there was no negative marking for getting an answer wrong). After the initial excitement, the family calmed down because, in the meanwhile, an alternative employment opportunity had arisen, and I was called for an interview for the prestigious Oberoi hotel management programme in Delhi in late June 1980. I cleared the preliminary selection rounds for this job and made it to the final stage, where the interview panel was chaired by P.R.S. ('Biki') Oberoi, the then Vice-Chairman of the Oberoi hotel chain and son of the legendary founder, Mohan Singh Oberoi.

A diversion into the hospitality sector

It was rumoured that unless one had some 'pull', it was impossible to get into the prestigious Oberoi hotel management programme. Since I had no pull whatsoever, I did not expect to get the job. But the unexpected happened: Mr Oberoi asked me what he probably considered to be a difficult question: 'Mr Iyer, I assume you know that Ronald Reagan has just become the Republican nominee for the upcoming US Presidential elections. But can you tell me the name of his Vice-Presidential running mate? Also, name two important positions held by him prior to this?' By an incredible stroke of fortune, I knew the answer to this rather obscure question, having recently read a newspaper article about it. 'Yes, sir,' I reeled off confidently. 'His name is George H.W. Bush and he was the CIA Director, and before that the Chief of the US Liasion Office to China.' This poised and correct answer floored the Chairman as well as other members of the panel, and I was selected as a management trainee in the Oberoi hotel management programme.

Pro-Tip: Never underestimate the power of being well read. Whether for examinations, interviews or even casual conversations, from newspapers to fiction to biographies, being well read will make you stand out.

Returning to Kanpur, some animated discussions ensued at home as to whether I should focus on spending the next four months (July–October 1980) studying for the civil services main exam or join the Oberoi hotel management programme in Delhi on 1 September. We all recognized the slim chances of my getting through the main exam to the interview stage, and then doing well enough in the interview to finally get selected for the top service, the IAS. The family consensus was that I should abandon the idea of sitting for the civil services main exam, which was a bird in the bush, and instead take the bird in hand, the Oberoi hotel job offer. To eliminate any potential vacillation between the two options, and to permanently close the option of writing the civil services main exam, I decided, rather dramatically, to tear up the application form which was due by 10 September 1980. Just before I could do so, however, my mother, with her usual presence of mind, snatched the application form from me, and stowed it safely away in the top drawer of the kitchen cabinet.

My hotel management career, which began on 1 September 1980, was short-lived. I quit after only 10 days. While I had started having second thoughts about the job after only a few days of exposure to the hospitality industry, it turned out that my father, originally the strongest proponent of a hotel management career, was also, in parallel, having a change of heart. The latter happened during a visit to Delhi on 9 September, after he shared a couple of drinks that evening with Air Commodore R.K. ('Tich') Nehru, an old military colleague, at the Air Force Central Vista mess on Janpath. No doubt in an expansive mood after the drinks flowed, the Air Commodore convinced my father that his son should sit for the civil services exam and abandon any idea of a career in hotel management. So, my father, rather sheepishly, came to meet me the next morning at the Oberoi Maidens hotel, where our training was going on.

Taking permission to skip a class on gourmet cutting of vegetables, I sat down with my dad at a nearby café and had a heart-to-heart chat about career options. 'Do you want to spend your life working for wealthy hotel guests or do you want to be a District Magistrate?' he asked. When he put it that way, the choice was clear – I preferred to be a District Magistrate. The only minor snag was that I had to get into the IAS first.

Returning to the chosen path

I pointed out to my father that even if I quit the Oberoi hotel job the same day, I would still have only two months to study for the civil services main exam, commencing in early November. 'That's okay,' said my ever-sanguine father. 'You can give it a full-fledged try next year. Take this year's main exam as a dress rehearsal.' He had strategically brought along the main exam application form with him, so we hurriedly filled it up and rushed to Dholpur House, the UPSC building on Shahjahan Road, and submitted the form just before the 5 p.m. deadline. I went back to Oberoi Maidens and informed the Course Director, P.S. Ajja, that I was quitting the programme with immediate effect.

My father and I returned to Kanpur the next day. I had exactly two months to prepare for the main exam, starting on 10 November 1980, and reviewing the extensive syllabus for the main exam was daunting. There were eight papers to be written: two papers each for both my chosen subjects, philosophy and English literature, both of which were at the master's level; two general studies papers; and a paper each on the English language and any other Indian language. The exam syllabus for English literature seemed vast because it was pegged at the master's level, while I only had a bachelor's degree. I also had little idea about philosophy at any level, let alone the master's. Further, my general knowledge was rudimentary at best although it had improved somewhat with my preparation for the preliminary exam. The only paper I was confident about doing well in was the English language paper, which was not of much use since, being only for qualifying purposes, it would not fetch me any marks. On the other hand, I was mortally afraid about failing the Hindi qualifying paper. On top of all these challenges, I had only two months to prepare for the main exam. With the odds stacked against me, I realized that there was no point panicking. With little to lose, I could afford to take a chance and try something different by way of preparation for the main exam.

Examination strategy

I needed to optimize my preparation time management and chalked out a 10-hours-daily studying schedule, seven days a week. The strategy I adopted was to (i) be extremely selective about topics to be studied, (ii) use any help I could get from others, and (iii) leverage my usually reliable memory to strategically deploy quotations from famous authors in my answers to examination questions. So, for my English literature papers, after poring over question papers from previous years, I decided to concentrate on only a third of the syllabus. It was all hands on deck, and my father even took a week's leave and prepared bullet points for me on answers to potential questions for the two philosophy papers, including information about an obscure topic called phenomenology, which neither of us had heard of before.

For the Hindi qualifying exam, I memorized a few Hindi essays, written in English by my dad and translated into Hindi by his PA, Mr Katiyar. Every Hindi essay I memorized, irrespective of topic, had the same opening sentence: '*Bachpan mein main Keral ke ek kasbe mein rehta tha.*' (In my childhood, I lived in a small town in Kerala.) The idea was to try to earn some brownie points from the exam paper evaluator on the grounds that even though I was from Kerala, in south India, and presumably did not know much Hindi, I was still courageously attempting a Hindi language paper. Hopefully, he or she would be generous enough to pass me. My general studies preparation, on the other hand, was thorough. I read up on the history and geography of

India, went through several newspapers a day and benefitted by becoming much more aware of the world around me.

> **Pro-Tip**: If you have your back against the wall, get creative and don't be afraid to try unconventional methods.

Sidestep when you need to

As it turned out, my unconventional preparation paid off. All the questions, including one on phenomenology, for which I had prepared answers turned up. However, in one of the English literature papers, I met my match with a question on 'The Lyricism of Coleridge' about which I did not know much. Rather than admitting defeat though, I decided to tackle the answer in a different way. Drawing upon my reasonably good memory, I quoted verbatim the following opening lines from 'Kubla Khan', one of Coleridge's most famous poems:

> *In Xanadu did Kubla Khan*
> *A stately pleasure dome decree*
> *Where Alph the sacred river ran*
> *Through caverns measureless to man*
> *Down to a sunless sea*

For good measure, I wrote something flowery about the 'throbbing intensity of Coleridge's alliteration', referring to the fact that the last two words of each of the first five opening lines of the poem began with the same letter, which led to a rhythmic cadence at the end of each line. Perhaps the examiner was impressed or perhaps I managed to confuse him or her. Either way, I did well in the English literature paper and even managed to pass the Hindi language exam.

To everybody's surprise, I cleared the civil services main exam and qualified for the interview stage. With my performance in interviews having improved since the 'inflation-deflation' fiasco, I was confident when appearing for what was known as the 'personality test' at the UPSC in Delhi in March 1981. My interview panel was headed by the then UPSC Chairman, Dr M.L. Shahare. Since I had studied for a year in the US after my bachelor's degree, the discussion focused mainly on life as a student in the US, for which I was well prepared. The interview lasted about 45 minutes and I came out feeling pretty good.

The final result of the UPSC examination was expected two months later. In the interim, I applied for and got selected as a sub-editor with the *Indian Express* in Delhi. One of the highlights of my brief stint there involved a meeting with the owner of the *Indian Express* and the grand old man of Indian journalism, Ramnath Goenka. The Executive Editor those days was Arun Shourie and he promised to shift me from the copy desk to a field journalist position soon. Alas, my spell at the newspaper was not to last long.

Three capital letters that changed my life – IAS

I had gone home to Kanpur on a few days' leave in early June 1981 and during this time, the rumour mill was in full swing, claiming that the final results of the civil services main exam were to come out any day. In those days the results were published in the Delhi newspapers and these reached Kanpur only the next day. My father decided to send one of his office staff to the nearby airport to request any random disembarking passenger to hand over their Delhi newspaper to check if the IAS results had been published. An obliging passenger handed over the *Indian Express* and it turned out that the civil services exam results had been published that very day.

My father came home a little earlier that day, bringing the newspaper with him. As I met him at the door, he simply said, 'You got it.' I jumped up with excitement and hit my head, quite hard, on the low ceiling. I had indeed got into the IAS and was ranked 81st overall. It was an exciting day for the family and we celebrated with my mother's delicious payasam. It was great to get into the IAS, India's premier civil service, but my predominant emotion was an overwhelming sense of relief that my persistent attempts at job-hunting had paid off and, in a sense, the best had been saved for the last.

2

Blunder when you are younger

FROM THE HILLS OF MUSSOORIE TO THE DOON VALLEY, AND
THEN TO LUCKNOW

THE FIRST FEW years of one's career are usually a combination of apprehension, fun, taking risks, making some foolish mistakes and hopefully learning from them. My early career more or less followed this pattern. One thing is for sure: if there is a quota for making mistakes throughout your career, it probably makes sense to commit most of the blunders as early as possible and get them out of your way.

The Harkidun trek – rubbing my peers the wrong way

The Foundation Course (FC) training at the Mussoorie Academy of about four months in 1981 consisted of 400 'probationers' (officer trainees) from all the Class I civil services. One of the mandatory exercises all probationers had to undergo was a seven-day trek. Our FC Course Director (CD), an inspirational and dynamic Indian Police Service (IPS) officer called S.H. Mohan, selected me as one of the trek team leaders. All of a sudden I was pitchforked into leading a team of about 20 probationers to a difficult (or so it seemed) trekking destination called Harkidun in the Garhwal Himalayas. The briefing for team leaders by the CD included a non-negotiable condition that all the team members had to make it to the final destination, which in our case was the Harkidun Forest Rest House at an altitude of about 11,000 ft.

I probably took the CD's instructions too seriously because I found myself at an impasse the evening before our trekking group's final 'assault' to Harkidun from Osla. This was a steep uphill stretch of about 12 km. The evening before the climb, which was to commence early the next morning, three of my team members came up to me and declared that they did not plan to trek up to Harkidun and would wait for us at Osla on our return instead.

It turned out to be quite a confrontation, with the 'ringleader' bluntly questioning my authority to insist on their making the climb. To overcome this stalemate, I decided to step back and enlist the support of my core team, a few like-minded, 'keen-type' trekkers. They were tasked with having one-on-one chats with the reluctant trekkers and persuading them to join the rest of us for the final climb.

These bilateral conversations, which went on late into the night, worked much better than the open confrontation I had had with the protesters earlier that evening. The three reluctant trekkers finally agreed to join the rest of us the next morning, and made the final climb, albeit with some difficulty. In the end, having reached the Harkidun Forest Rest House, they were proud of their achievement and, today, almost 40 years later, they are all good friends of mine.

> **Pro-Tip:** It is important in any job to develop a core group of like-minded supporters who can step in during difficult situations and open informal back-channels with your 'opponents' to resolve problems.

Returning to Mussoorie, each trek team leader had to provide feedback on his or her trek to their 400 batchmates in the Academy's auditorium, the Sardar Patel Hall. After giving them a brief description of our trek, I ended by saying that while we had had a great time, our team members had got fed up of the **4 Ps** over the course of the week-long trek: Parathas, Potatoes, Pickle and ... Parameswaran! It raised the expected laugh but I was not sure if the dissenters in my trekking team were equally amused.

Beginning life as an administrator

Allocated the Uttar Pradesh (UP) cadre, after my training in Mussoorie, I was sent to Gorakhpur in eastern UP for my district training. I was fortunate to have a very welcoming District Magistrate (DM) named B.M. Vohra to supervise my training. He was an outstanding athlete, had captained St. Xavier's College, Bombay (now Mumbai), in cricket and had also been Sunil Gavaskar's captain. My first evening in Gorakhpur district was memorable: I was staying at the Gorakhpur University guest house and Mr Vohra, himself driving the DM's white ambassador car with a blue light flashing on top, came to collect me and take me for dinner at the house of the Superintendent of Police, P.C. Sabharwal.

It turned out to be a *teen patti* (the Indian version of poker, each player being dealt three cards) party. The rules were pretty basic. I easily picked them up and soon embarked on a long, losing streak. At a time when my monthly salary was about Rs 700, I had lost close to Rs 300, a princely sum in those days, when the *teen patti* party wound up. Driving me back to the guest house, Mr Vohra, who had won about Rs 500 that evening, mainly from me, very kindly offered to return my losses. I politely refused, saying that a loss was a loss and I hoped to win the next time. Since then I have continued to consistently lose in *teen patti* sessions with batchmates over the years during Diwali parties that my wife and I have attended, but have always been ahead of the game due to the old saying – 'unlucky at cards, lucky in love'.

The *teen patti* loss was minimal in the overall scheme of things, but it gave me an early clue about how to conduct myself after a defeat. There will always be losses and wins in one's life and career but what counts is how you handle them. We earn the respect of others if we know how to take our losses. In the immortal words of the great poet–novelist Rudyard Kipling, from his poem 'If', one should look at both 'triumph and disaster' as 'imposters' and treat them both 'just the same'. I surely had more than my fair share of disasters in the early years of my career, none more than in my first regular job as the Sub Divisional Magistrate (SDM) in Dehradun district, in the then undivided state of Uttar Pradesh. Some of these disasters were of my own making, I concede, but since we all make mistakes, it's better to be reckless earlier and get it out of the way, rather than later in your career, when the stakes are much higher.

Chalking up my first blunder

Early in my stint as SDM Dehradun, I was catapulted to the headlines of the local newspaper for all the wrong reasons. This episode pertained to the illicit limestone quarrying in the hills of Mussoorie. In a way this was the beginning of environmental activism in India. A group called Rural Litigation and Entitlement Kendra, Dehradun, had filed a writ petition in the Supreme Court of India, seeking cancellation of the limestone quarry leases in the hills of Mussoorie and also the immediate stopping of all ongoing mining operations, usually conducted through blasting of dynamite. Justice P.N. Bhagwati of the Supreme Court endorsed the plaint and all mining was technically stopped through the court's order. It fell upon the district administration, that is, SDM Dehradun, to enforce the said order.

I took this task very seriously and would often travel at night in my Mahindra jeep to the Mussoorie hills to make sure there was no illicit dynamite blasting at the closed limestone quarries. I usually drove by myself, with a couple of police constables in tow. While I was mostly successful in enforcing the court's order, I may have overdone it once. On one late-night trip, while driving in the upper Mussoorie hills, near a limestone quarry belonging to a prominent mine owner, I came upon a *gattu* (mini truck) carrying freshly mined limestone. Excited to have caught them red-handed, I stopped the truck and arrested both the driver and his helper. Impressive, right? I thought so too. It turned out, however, that they had a special permit for removing the residual limestone already quarried, and that I had wrongly arrested them.

'*SDM Dehradun Plunges Administration into a Mess*' screamed the banner headlines of the local newspaper *Himachal Star*, which, incidentally, was owned by the limestone quarry owners' association. The newspaper had many harsh words to say about my 'reckless and irresponsible behaviour' but the saving grace was the consistent support of S.K. Das, the DM and my boss. He was very understanding and said something to me that I have always remembered: 'It's fine, Iyer. It's okay to make a bona fide mistake. We expect young officers to take bold decisions, even if some of them go wrong.'

Perhaps I took him a little too literally, because I made many more 'bold decisions' in my two-year stint as SDM Dehradun, going full throttle after the local crooks and land mafia with varying degrees of success (and failure). These included 'attaching' (taking over) the Madhuban Hotel on Rajpur Road, the best in Dehradun at the time, for non-payment of sales tax dues and appointing G.B. Patnaik, the Managing Director of the Garhwal Mandal Vikas Nigam, as the receiver (the manager). This ploy worked well and the sales tax dues were paid immediately by the furious owner of the hotel. I also shut down the huge ARC cement factory, which was spewing smoke and dust and polluting the fragile ecosystem of the Doon valley, through an order under Section 133/139 (removal of public nuisance) of the Code of Criminal Procedure. This tactic failed, though, since the District and Sessions Judge revoked my order on appeal by the ARC cement factory owner.

Meeting Mrs Indira Gandhi

It was during my posting as SDM Dehradun that I met Prime Minister (PM) Indira Gandhi. She had come to Dehradun on Diwali day, 24 October 1984, along with Mrs Teji Bachchan (mother of Amitabh Bachchan) to spend the festival with her grandchildren and their friends. While the PM and her entourage relaxed on the spacious lawns of the iconic Circuit House of

Dehradun and lit Diwali firecrackers in the early evening, the DM, the PM's chief security officer and I stood at a distance. At the end of the day, the PM graciously thanked each of us before departing by helicopter from the Gurkha Training Centre. Little did I know that only a week later, on 31 October, she would be assassinated by her own Sikh bodyguards at her residence in Delhi. Her death had repercussions for me even in sleepy Dehradun.

In the aftermath of Mrs Gandhi's assassination, riots against Sikhs broke out across the country, especially in north India. There was an immediate backlash against the Sikhs of Dehradun. The well-known Moti Mahal restaurant, owned by a Sikh gentleman, was burnt down despite our efforts to maintain law and order in the town. One evening at about 7 p.m. in the days following the assassination, while on patrol in the Prem Nagar area (near the Indian Military Academy), I saw that a rapidly gathering unruly mob was signalling its intent to burn down the house of a prominent Sikh member of the community. Using the loudspeaker fixed to the front of my jeep, I called out to the mob to stand back but they refused and began to hurl lighted torches at the house. When I saw some members of the Sikh family stranded on their balcony, I quickly decided to order my two armed police constables to fire warning shots to prevent the mob from burning down the house and likely killing its inhabitants.

During our law and order classes at the Academy, we were taught to order firing only in situations where other preventive measures had failed. The instructions in such dire situations were to shoot to kill. In the moment, however, I disregarded this advice and shouted at my two constables: '*Hawa mein fire karo*.' (Fire in the air.) Pulling out their ancient 303 Lee-Enfield rifles, they fired upwards, well above the mob. Fortunately, no one was injured and the tactic worked. Once the firing started, the mob broke up in panic and rapidly dispersed. I was in a sweat, but the house and its inhabitants were saved.

In a slightly bizarre sequel to this episode, the two constables came to meet me in my office the next morning and asked for written orders for the previous evening's firing. It turned out that their boss, the Reserve Inspector (RI) at the Police Lines, had demanded a written order, 'back-dated' to the previous day, from the SDM to replenish the bullets expended by the constables. While it seemed odd to me to issue such a back-dated written order for the previous evening, I went with the flow, and duly wrote out a quasi-judicial 'firing order' which enabled them to replenish their bullets.

In the meantime, as some looting of shops and sporadic attacks on Sikhs continued, I, along with my seasoned Deputy Superintendent of Police (DSP), camped at the Prem Nagar police station. We soon rounded up and arrested about 20 miscreants identified as being responsible for the looting and violence. Most of them already had criminal histories as corroborated by the Prem Nagar police station's 'history sheeters' register (the list of habitual offenders maintained by every police station).

The news of the arrest of the rioters spread in the neighbourhood and had an immediate calming effect on the law and order situation. Since the main jail in Dehradun was already overflowing with arrested rioters, we had to keep our 20 history-sheeters in the Prem Nagar police station lock-up for a couple of days. The only problem was that it became difficult to feed them using the meagre diet allowance of less than a rupee a day per prisoner permitted under the British era *Jail Manual*. A creative solution soon emerged with the wives and mothers of the history-sheeters volunteering to come forward and set up a *langar* (food camp) in the police station premises to feed their family members. They ended up feeding more than those 20 men, with the police personnel happily tucking into the hot meals cooked by the kind ladies. Even the DSP and I joined in for some delicious parathas, sabzi and daal.

Unsuccessfully running a bus corporation

After spending close to two years in Dehradun, I was transferred to Lucknow in July 1985 as General Manager of the UP State Road Transport Corporation (UPSRTC). The UPSRTC was a mammoth organization with about 50,000 employees and operating over 5,000 buses on both short-haul and long-distance routes. It had incurred huge financial losses, so the government decided to overhaul its management, bringing a new team to run it. My immediate boss was the dynamic Keshav Varma, an IAS officer on secondment to UP from the Gujarat cadre.

On the advice of an expert team of transport management consultants, we decided to restructure the corporation into nine decentralized business/profit centres on the lines of the Pallavan Transport Corporation in Tamil Nadu. It made sense conceptually but we had not reckoned with opposition from the 50,000 employees and the six major unions which represented them. The unions were dead against the restructuring idea and, despite the hundreds of hours of negotiations, we failed to get them on board. The restructuring plan was finally shelved, and I later realized I had forgotten the lesson from my Mussoorie trek about having a core team that could open back channels of communication with the 'opposers'. In this situation, having a small UPSRTC team of experienced and credible officers open informal, behind-the-scenes parleys with targeted trade union leaders may have helped in breaking the deadlock.

An excellent memory from my short stint at the UPSRTC, however, was tracking my father, by now an Air Marshal, and his team of over 150 Air Force and civilian runners on an incredible 250 km run from Agra to Delhi in just three and a half days. My father was a marathon runner, a gold medallist at the World Veteran Games in Singapore in 1981, and an ultra-fitness fanatic, who clocked anywhere from 15 km to 20 km on a daily basis. Even today, at the ripe old age of 91, he jogs for 10 km a day and has covered over 1,20,000 km in his running career. In 1985, at the age of 56, he decided to take a group of runners all the way from Agra to Delhi. Starting out on 5 October, he planned to reach his destination on 8 October – Air Force Day. Although proud of my dad's 'crazy' idea, I wisely decided not to emulate him and, instead, followed him for sections of the journey in a UPSRTC bus! I was there at hand at the Air Force sports stadium at Palam, Delhi, when he led his merry band of runners, many of whom had dropped out along the way, before a cheering audience and presented the Air Force flag to a beaming Air Chief Marshal Denis La Fontaine.

My run-in with Mr T.N. Seshan

With the excitement of the Agra–Delhi run over and thinking that I would benefit from some policy experience in the Lucknow Secretariat, I requested a transfer from the UPSRTC and was posted as Joint Secretary (JS), Department of Environment, in the UP Government. I learned a great deal here, both about the environment but also about time management, from my boss, Kamal Pande, the Secretary, Department of Environment. The IAS topper of the 1965 batch, he would later become the Cabinet

Secretary of India. Mr Pande was a stickler for punctuality and would arrive at office on the dot at 10 a.m., the start of the work day, and leave sharp at 5 p.m., when office hours ended (we had a six-day week in those days). He left no work unfinished and no file undisposed during the working day – something that I have tried to emulate throughout my career. Initially a little distant, Mr Pande became a great friend and mentor and taught me the importance of 'travelling light' – avoiding pomposity and not taking oneself too seriously. Under him, I learned the value of punctuality, cutting to the chase and keeping meetings and conversations short.

> **Pro-Tip:** Remember, you have only about 30 seconds before you lose your audience's interest. Get to the point.

Working in the Secretariat, with none of the fabled perks traditionally associated with IAS officers, I used to commute to office by bicycle, evoking pity and even contempt from some of my batchmates, who were mostly posted in public sector corporations or directorates, where they had adequate *gadi-ghoda* (literally 'car-horse', but referring here to the perks of office) to make life comfortable. So, I made a virtue out of necessity and, in consequence, learned about the advantages of doing one's job efficiently regardless of the perks, keeping my head down and letting my work speak for itself.

During my time in the Secretariat at the Department of Environment, I discovered that one could actually do something different, even potentially risky, in a supposedly staid and boring desk job. Fortunately, there was something interesting to sink my teeth into. The then new Environment (Protection) (EP) Act of 1986 had just been enacted by Parliament. I became interested in the new Act, which superseded the erstwhile Air and Water Pollution Acts, and spent a great deal of time studying and analysing it. My take on the new Act was that while it took a far more comprehensive approach to tackling all aspects of environmental pollution, including air, water and even noise, than earlier Acts, the powers to regulate pollution were over-centralized, with inadequate delegation to the states.

With the audacity (and foolhardiness) of youth, I then ventured to write an op-ed about the new Act, and sent it off to the *Times of India*. To my surprise, they actually published it. I felt a sense of pride at having a serious article on a substantive topic published in the largest circulated national daily. The pride was soon punctured, however, when I received a call from Sidharth Behura, the Staff Officer to the Chief Secretary. A little apprehensive, I went to his office on the ground floor of the Secretariat Annexe. 'Take a look at this letter,' he said. I read the letter with growing concern. It was a nasty one, a 'stinker' in fact, from T.N. Seshan, Secretary, Ministry of Environment; he would later become the Cabinet Secretary of India and, subsequently, the Chief Election Commissioner. The letter was addressed to his IAS batchmate, J.K. Kalyanakrishnan, the Chief Secretary of UP. Mr Seshan was furious about my article and his letter to the Chief Secretary ended with a recommendation to take strict action against the officer (me) for criticizing government policy.

While the most 'critical' aspect of my article was the title – 'A Critical Look at Environment Act' – not given by me but by the *Times of India* editor, I have to admit I had also written in the op-ed that 'while the new act is fairly comprehensive in nature, there are nonetheless some drawbacks in it'. I was asked to meet the Chief Secretary. Expecting the sky to fall on my head, I started blurting out my explanation to the Chief Secretary as soon as I entered his huge room. He stopped me midway, smiled and silently handed me a piece of paper. Thinking that this was my suspension order or worse, I warily glanced at the document, and immediately calmed down. It was a letter from him to Mr Seshan, saying that the UP Government in fact encouraged young officers to analyse and deconstruct important Acts like the EP Act from an implementation perspective. The Chief Secretary had ended his response with: 'We encourage young officers to think about such important subjects and even write about them, and I am sure that you will agree with me.' I was amazed at the large-heartedness of Mr Kalyanakrishnan, who had not even bothered to ask whether I had taken formal permission to write the article. There was apparently no further response from Mr Seshan.

It is safe to say that without the support of seniors like Mr Pande and Mr Kalyanakrishnan, the early years of my career would not have been such a time of learning and maturing. If you are a team leader, even as you keep one eye on their activities, allow the youngsters in your team some amount of space and freedom to ideate, take a few risks, and perhaps even blunder, but protect them if things go wrong.

My first tryst with Bollywood

Interspersed with the stumbles in the Department of Environment were some fun times too, especially our attempt at producing a Bollywood-style movie, called *Vasundhara*, on the theme of the environment. This was a great break from the mostly file-pushing work in the dull Secretariat. Anuj Bishnoi, the topper of our 1981 batch, had dropped by my little cubicle of an office in the

Secretariat that I shared with another officer. Over a cup of tea, I casually mentioned to him that we were thinking of producing a documentary film on the theme of environmental protection. He scoffed at the idea and suggested that we instead make a full-fledged Bollywood-esque feature film on the same theme, which people would actually watch. A great idea, I thought, and, to my delight, so did my boss.

I plunged into the task of identifying a film director and selecting the cast with him. We ended up hiring Ashok Ahuja (who had just made the movie *Aadharshila*) as our producer-director, and casting Naseeruddin Shah, Neena Gupta, Benjamin Gilani, Tom Alter and a few others. The film was loosely based on the story of our anti-limestone quarrying movement in Dehradun when I was the SDM. I found the process of making the film much more exciting than the final product, to be honest. The film was shown just once on Doordarshan and probably never saw the light of day again! Anuj had the last laugh, as good friends often do, saying that not only was the movie a flop but, in selecting only 'art-movie' actors and actresses, I had squandered a prime opportunity to hobnob with Bollywood superstars.

These early years in the IAS were the time for me to take risks, to do foolish things, to innovate and to make mistakes – big and small. These are usually forgiven early in one's career and provide invaluable lessons. So, my advice, for what it is worth, is to go for broke early in your career: the lessons you will learn, whether you succeed or fail, will come in very handy later.

3

Play the hand you are dealt

BEING SHUFFLED AND RESHUFFLED IN THE GOVERNMENT
OF INDIA

IN ANY CAREER, there are ups and downs. But every time you feel you're in a poor job or situation, and that you've been dealt a hand you don't like, remember that you can always play it smart and gain a lot from the experience. I went through a few of these seemingly not-so-optimal situations during my term with the Government of India in Delhi from 1987 to 1992 and, while I may not have realized it at the time, I ended up learning something useful from each one of them.

In the battle zone

In December 1986, just when I was settling in at the Department of Environment, Government of UP, Lucknow, I was sounded out about becoming the Private Secretary (PS) to Arun Singh, the Minister of State for Defence in the Government of India, Delhi. At that time, I had only about five years of service and it was rather unusual to go on deputation to the Government of India so early in one's career. I was called to Delhi to meet Mr Singh, who was reported to be one of PM Rajiv Gandhi's closest friends. He asked me if I was interested in becoming his PS and spoke about the incredible exposure I would get as PS to the Union Minister of State for Defence. In addition, he said that I would have, at an early stage of my career, a bird's-eye view of how the Government of India worked. It sounded like an exciting job, especially as it meant working with people in high places, and I did not need too much convincing. I thanked the Minister for his offer and immediately conveyed my acceptance. Boarding the overnight Lucknow Mail train to Delhi on 31 December 1986, I fittingly took up my new job at the Defence Ministry on the first day of the new year.

I could not meet the boss, as I came to refer to Mr Singh, on 1 January 1987 since he did not believe in coming to office on New Year's Day. Instead, I went around the Defence Ministry offices at South Block and called on the senior officers of the Ministry. The job of PS was very different from anything I had done before. I now had to run the Minister's office and also act as his executive assistant. My roles included managing his calendar, preparing briefs for him, deciphering his usually unintelligible handwritten notes, and going through all the files that came to him with a fine-tooth comb, then putting them up to him for clearance. The fact that many of the Defence Ministry files were marked 'Top Secret' made the job all the more exciting, albeit challenging. Mr Singh also set a very high standard in terms of office efficiency, as I was soon to find out.

Early in my new job, I was called in by the boss, who wanted to know why a particular file was still pending in our office. When I said I had yet to review it, he bluntly told me that I had better get my act together since he believed in a 24-hour file clearance policy. Coming from the more leisurely pace of the Lucknow Secretariat, I had to rapidly adjust to this more rigorous schedule. The boss was also in the habit of issuing rapid-fire instructions to me and, one day early in my tenure, noticed I was just nodding without writing anything down because I did not have a notebook with me. 'Mr Iyer,' he said sarcastically, 'I am sure you have a photographic memory and can remember everything I am telling you, but do me a favour and always bring a notebook and pen when you meet me, and at least pretend to write things down.' I never forgot to carry a notebook (or an iPad in more modern times) with me for meetings throughout my career.

> **Pro-Tip:** Always take notes, no matter how confident you are that you will remember everything.

Back to Mr Seshan

I quickly settled into the job as PS to the Minister and, very soon, had an interesting, though somewhat unsettling, experience.

Mr Singh decided to call a meeting of the senior officers of the departments concerned to review the security arrangements for the Republic Day parade on 26 January 1987. T.N. Seshan was now Secretary (Security) in the Cabinet Secretariat and he arrived for the meeting a few minutes before schedule. Coming into my room, and having seen my name on the wall outside my room, he smiled at me and asked if I was the same officer who had written 'that very perceptive' newspaper article on the Environment (Protection) Act, 1986. I was understandably nervous at meeting Mr Seshan in the flesh but, surprisingly, he seemed very friendly. When I took him into my Minister's office, he smiled at my boss and said, 'Sir, you have no doubt selected a very bright young officer as your PS but, given his interest in the subject of environment, it might have been better if he had been posted to the Ministry of Environment.' My jaw dropped at this sudden change of heart and the Minister looked surprised. When I explained the story to him after the meeting, he laughed, and said, 'I'm not surprised at all. As my PS, you are probably someone he may like to keep in good humour.' I quickly learnt that positions of perceived power, such as PS to an important Minister, attract praise. Although it feels good to have famous or powerful people praise you, it is important to keep your feet firmly on the ground.

The Bofors story

In early April 1987, Swedish Radio broke what would come to be known as the Bofors story. The allegation was that the Swedish manufacturers of the Bofors 88 mm artillery gun, purchased by the Defence Ministry for the Indian Army, had paid an illegal commission to a middleman who had helped to secure the deal. Arun Singh, whose integrity was beyond doubt, and who had overseen the process of procuring the Bofors gun well before I had joined his office, was furious with the Swedish Radio broadcast. 'This is complete nonsense,' he declared. 'There is no question of any commission being paid in this deal.' He proceeded to brilliantly defend it in Parliament. My main role during the Parliamentary debates was to supply Strepsils (cough lozenges) to my Minister who had developed a very sore throat as a result of his many speeches in both the Lok Sabha and the Rajya Sabha.

I remember that period well because I had just got engaged to be married to Indira, daughter of Air Commodore R. Gopalaswami, who was working as an advisor to the Scientific Advisor to the Defence Minister. Indira and I had met at the Rashtrapati Bhawan investiture ceremony where our respective fathers were being honoured by the President of India with the Ati Vishisht Seva Medal. Something must have clicked between us in that brief encounter over chai and samosas at the post-awards tea party, because I found myself at her house in Moti Bagh the very next evening. It took only a few days of driving around Delhi in the ancient jeep which I had borrowed from a colleague for us to conclude that we were in love with each other and wanted to get married. The next step, however, as determined by our respective parents, was for us to get engaged, which, as it turned out, was conducted 'in absentia'. Indira's parents went to Nagpur to meet my parents and the four of them carried out a sort of engagement ceremony, while my fiancée and I went out for dinner at a revolving restaurant in the Asian Games Village at Siri Fort.

Soon after getting engaged, Indira and I were invited to Arun Singh's house for dinner at 9, Race Course Road (today known as 9, Lok Kalyan Marg). During the dinner, Mr Singh received a phone call from Prabhu Chawla, a well-known journalist, who asked him if he was planning to resign soon, which Mr Singh denied. And then, in the middle of July, Mr Singh indeed decided to quit. He typed out his resignation letter on his portable typewriter, sealed it and asked me to hand it over to Vincent George, Private Secretary to the PM. Mr Singh was thereafter called for a one-on-one meeting with the PM, after which his resignation was formally accepted. Returning from his meeting with the PM, Mr Arun Singh's instructions to me were: 'Clear out the office and wind up by this evening.' It took my team and me over six hours to complete the task; it was midnight by the time we were done. I had worked as his PS for a short period of six and a half months.

Up-skilling from an official high to a personal high

Once Arun Singh resigned, I was left without a job and had to choose between returning to Uttar Pradesh, my home cadre, and taking up a desk job in the vast Defence Ministry. Many colleagues advised me to return to UP since it would be a big comedown to transition from a coveted and high-profile position as PS to a powerful Minister to the boring job of an Under Secretary in the Department of Defence Production. I chose the latter, however, not least because I had a personal interest in staying on in Delhi. With the high-pressure job of a PS now a thing of the past, this was a great opportunity to spend time with Indira prior to our wedding planned for September 1987. The wedding, south Indian-style at the Sankara Mandap in Vasant Vihar, was attended mainly by family on both sides, but Mrs and Mr Arun Singh also came and enjoyed the traditional wedding breakfast served on a banana leaf. The wedding reception at the Air Force Officers' Mess on Zakir Hussain Marg was attended by friends, colleagues and family, along with a large defence contingent, including all the three military chiefs.

Taking full advantage of my low-key desk job in the Department of Defence Production, I was thrilled to be able to take long lunch breaks, eating chole bhature with my wife at India International Centre (IIC) and going for walks in the nearby Lodhi Garden. We chose IIC as the place to meet since Indira was then working as a research economist at the adjacent Indian Council for Research on International Economic Relations. It also helped that I had an understanding boss in J.N. Kaul, Additional Secretary in the Department of Defence Production, who was fine with my long lunch breaks as long as I delivered on my work, such as it was.

It was on Indira's advice during that time that I took 15 months' leave to do an MBA under the National Management Programme at the Management Development Institute, Gurgaon. Herself armed with a master's in economics from the Delhi School of Economics, Indira felt that it would be useful for me, while still in service, to acquire a professional degree in management. It turned out to be a great idea, enabling me to complement my practical experience with an understanding of the latest management concepts. This new MBA programme was meant for public or private sector executives with at least five years of work experience, and had been specially designed by India's premier management institutes, the Indian Institutes of Management. The package included having their top professors teach us. However, the highlight of this period for Indira and me was the birth of our daughter, Tara. Since Indira did most of the hard work in looking after the baby, I managed to stay relatively focused on my MBA studies and benefitted enormously from the programme. There was also a policy incentive for all those who achieved an overall A grade – such as myself – to get assigned to an economic ministry. I was posted to the Ministry of Textiles after earning my MBA and found my MBA training very useful as I navigated the policy and economic space in the textile sector.

Wild mail chase at the Ministry of Textiles

I joined as Under Secretary in the Ministry of Textiles in November 1989 and was placed in the division responsible for managing the government's policy, including industrial licensing matters, for promoting the production of textile yarn. My immediate superior was Dr J.N. Chaubey, JS in charge of the division. While he brought an economist's perspective to the industrial licensing sector, I learned the nitty-gritty of the job – the criteria and process for the evaluation and recommendation of industrial licence applications – from my extremely competent Section Officer, Oma Nand. But even Oma Nand's competence could not prevent a blunder concerning the renewal of a polyester yarn manufacturing licence for one of the most well-known industrial houses in India.

The usually routine matter of renewing a manufacturing licence turned out to be a comedy of errors and led to a wild 'mail' chase around Lutyens' Delhi. Following the established practice, after obtaining the approval of the Secretariat of Industrial Approvals, the Section had put up the file to the JS through me, the Under Secretary. After the JS had signed off on it, the file was returned to the Section and the renewal letter issued. Almost immediately thereafter, Oma Nand came to me and said, 'Sir, we made a minor mistake in issuing that licence renewal letter; the term of the renewal should have been limited to a fixed period which we forgot to mention in the letter.' I told him that it was okay and we could issue a simple corrigendum. 'But let us inform the JS first,' I told Oma Nand.

When we informed Dr Chaubey of the turn of events, he blanched and seemed very concerned. 'Has the renewal letter actually been despatched?' he asked. 'Any corrigendum we plan to issue should get the approval of the Secretary. In the meanwhile, let's try to retrieve the renewal letter.' It turned out that the letter had already been sent by the dispatcher for mailing. The JS decided that we should try to recover it from the mailbox outside Udyog Bhawan, so the three of us rushed out and reached the mailbox. We soon found out that it was difficult, if not impossible (and probably illegal), to retrieve a letter from a mailbox.

Dr Chaubey was not going to give up so easily and decided to drag us to the main post office where mail was aggregated and then dispatched to the final destination. The main post office turned out to be Gol Dak Khana near the Central Secretariat and opposite the well-known girls' school, Convent of Jesus and Mary. The JS, Oma Nand and I went into the post office where there were huge piles of letters lying around amidst bustling activity. We met the Head Postmaster, a harried looking man, and the JS asked him if we could retrieve our 'important' letter before it was sent to its final destination. The Postmaster was at first incredulous and then amused. He said that even if he could retrieve our letter from the thousands lying around, it was completely illegal to intercept letters like this. He quoted some section from the Indian Posts and Telegraphs Act and said that we would need written authorization from the 'competent authority' to proceed.

Dr Chaubey was getting more and more desperate now and almost waded randomly into a huge pile of letters to look for ours, but finally decided against it. 'Let's go and meet the Member Posts in the Department of Posts and Telegraphs,' he told the two of us. So, we trooped off to that office, just off Parliament Street. The Member Posts was quite amused to hear our story and told my JS: 'My dear Chaubey, I must compliment your effort, but have to tell you that what you are asking for is well-nigh impossible. There is a quasi-judicial process for this kind of thing, it involves a lot of paperwork and takes a lot of time.'

It was now about 7.30 p.m. and my JS was getting fed up of the whole thing. His initial enthusiasm having waned considerably, he resignedly asked us to 'wind up'. Since the

Department of Posts and Telegraphs was very near my Curzon Road apartment, I suggested we all go there and have a cup of tea. Indira produced her special ginger tea for the guests and Dr Chaubey and Oma Nand finally relaxed. 'Well, it turned out to be a fruitless effort,' said the JS. 'Not much can be done now, let's figure it out tomorrow.' Oma Nand and I were a little apprehensive the following morning when we met the JS, wondering what his next move would be, but it turned out that he had forgotten about the whole thing and was already focused on something else.

> **Pro-Tip:** A smart survival policy is to keep your immediate boss in good humour even if what he or she proposes is a bit mad! Live to fight another day.

Striking a 'shirty' deal

After a year of working in the licencing division and completing the required nine years of service, I was promoted from Under Secretary to Deputy Secretary in the same Ministry. Having earned my spurs in the licensing division and now considered 'experienced' enough, I was given charge of the more important Export Division. India has traditionally been one of the major textiles and garments exporting countries in the world, and it was a fascinating task to assist my new JS, S. Narayanan, in framing and managing the national textiles and garments export policy in order to make the sector more globally competitive. Early in my tenure, a crisis occurred. India's exports of a garment category called 'tailored collar shirts' were suddenly embargoed in Canada, a major importing country. This apparently was on account of India exceeding its 'quota' in this garment category under the bilateral agreement between our two countries. The Canadian customs had, therefore, put a hard stop to the entry of these shirts into their country. It was early December 1990, the peak pre-Christmas shopping season in Canada, and both our garment exporters and their corresponding importers were in full-blown panic at this sudden and unexpected embargo.

Since my JS was out of the country at the time, the Secretary, R.K. Dar, instructed me to proceed immediately to Canada and 'sort this out'. I reached Ottawa in the second week of December in freezing weather and commenced negotiations the next morning with my Canadian counterpart, Jean St Jacques, from the Foreign Trade Department, to try and secure the release of our embargoed tailored collar shirts. Mr St Jacques, from Quebec, was a seasoned negotiator unlike me, a novice at this bilateral game. The negotiations were very formal and we made little headway.

It turned out that some of the 'export certificates' (allotted to the garment exporters' part of the quota) had been forged, and a large quantity of tailored collar shirts had already been illegally exported from India to Canada by unscrupulous exporters. This was what had caused the breaching of the overall 'national quota' ceiling for this product, leaving the genuine holders of the tailored collar shirt 'quota' stranded. Mr St Jacques refused to consider allowing the imports from genuine quota holders because, technically, India's total export 'quota' in this category had already been exceeded.

The formal negotiations broke for lunch and, after we ate a bland sandwich-and-soup meal, Mr St Jacques suggested that we take a walk on the frozen Ottawa river near his office. He had become quite friendly over the brief lunch break when we had exchanged notes about our respective lives and families. It turned out that he was an ice hockey fan and I, of course, was a passionate aficionado of all sports, especially tennis. As we chatted while strolling on the frozen river, Mr St Jacques gently hinted that there could be a way out of the negotiation impasse: while India had exceeded its quota of tailored collar shirts, it was under-exporting another category of garments – ladies' blouses. The Canadians were, therefore, willing to allow us to take a 'swing' from the unutilized category into the over-utilized category so that the overall numbers of the two categories remained the same. Mr St Jacques smiled and said that this was only his informal advice and I should formally propose this solution when negotiations resumed after lunch. He would then 'agree' to consider it after receiving approval from his 'competent authority'.

And, so it happened. When we returned to the negotiating table, I formally proposed a swing of 2,00,000 underutilized quota of ladies' blouses to the tailored collar shirts category. Jean St Jacques had obviously got his clearance from his competent authority already, for he promptly agreed to our proposal. I transmitted the message home and our exporters were able to get their products through Canadian customs and meet their Christmas shopping deadlines. Clearly, in this case, striking a deal off the negotiating table was more effective than concluding an agreement during the formal talks, and this has been my experience in most subsequent cases. Much later, when I received formal training for negotiations, I learned the term BATNA (Best Alternate to a Negotiated Agreement), and realized that Jean St Jacques and I had already stumbled upon a BATNA-type agreement in Ottawa during that winter of 1990.

While I had not taken my work as an Under Secretary in the Department of Defence Production very seriously, I dived deep into the intricacies of textiles and garments export policy at the Ministry of Textiles. I studied the then prevalent General Agreement on Trade and Tariffs, proposed improvements in India's quota policy and always prepared detailed negotiation briefs prior to bilateral negotiations with our major importing countries. One's work usually speaks for itself and it was good to become known as someone who could be relied upon to deliver quality output.

In June 1992 my deputation tenure in the Government of India ended and it was time to return to UP for my mandatory 'cooling off'*. In retrospect, from a conventional career perspective, I probably came to Delhi to work in the Government of India too soon, with only about five years of service. But I have no regrets, especially since I met and married my wife there. From a professional point of view, I found that attempting to specialize in a particular sector, such as textiles and garments exports, earns you the respect of others and could also pay dividends in the future. I also learned that while one has little control over where one is posted, the crucial thing is to make the best of the situation and try to convert any hand one is dealt into a winning one.

---

* An IAS officer is expected to return to his state cadre after completing his central deputation tenure in the Government of India – colloquially referred to as 'cooling off'.

4

Walk the straight and narrow

ADVENTURES OF A DISTRICT MAGISTRATE

EVERYONE USUALLY HAS to face ethical dilemmas in their career and in their lives. I faced more than my fair share of these during my stint as the DM in Bijnor district, Uttar Pradesh. My stint as DM Bijnor included quite a few intense experiences but, one way or another, I always landed on my feet.

Every IAS officer looks forward to becoming a DM, also known as District Collector and in some states Deputy Commissioner, a job which is usually considered the most memorable in one's career. There are today more than 700 districts in India, each with an average population of about 2 million people. The DM's job is to maintain law and order in his or her district, manage its development and, rather anachronistically, collect the land and miscellaneous revenues owed to the government. Even in this day and age, the DM is considered the *mai-baap* (literally mother and father, but figuratively a responsible caretaker) to all the people in the district, and is usually called upon to solve any and all problems within his or her jurisdiction. Without a doubt, it is one of the most challenging and fascinating jobs in the world!

DM Bijnor

Most of my IAS batchmates from the UP cadre had already become DMs by 1991 while I was still on deputation to the Government of India. So, after finishing my tenure in Delhi in June 1992, I was keen to get back to my cadre and become a DM. I received my posting orders as DM Bijnor in late June 1992. Bijnor is a district in western UP, a four-hour drive from Delhi. I took up my new job on 2 July 1992.

The DM's car was sent to Delhi early in the morning, and it was indeed exciting to make the drive to Bijnor from our Kasturba Gandhi Marg apartment near India Gate. With the family – now with an addition, our son, Venkat, who was born in July 1991 – set to join me later, I drove through Meerut, Muzaffarnagar and Khatauli before arriving at Bijnor, a small and sleepy town, and then through to the DM's residence. I was received with a smart salute from the sentry on guard at the entrance and we then slowly drove through a long, winding driveway up to the portico outside the DM's residence. The house itself was more than 150 years old, inhabited by successive DMs, from the days of the British Raj – a magnificent double-storey, circular building with large rooms. There was a huge estate outside, about 13 acres, with every conceivable type of fruit tree growing in it. Walking around the grounds, I discovered an ancient swimming pool and, to my delight, a somewhat dilapidated tennis court. Parked in the driveway were four Ambassador cars, all of which, apparently, were being used by my predecessor.

Setting out on the right foot

'Why are there so many cars here?' I asked Harish, my PA (private assistant or 'Steno-Babu' as all PAs are known in UP). The reply was, 'Sir, the first one is the DM's official car, the second one is also yours in your capacity as Chairman of the Zila Parishad, the third is from the Small Savings Department and the fourth is from the Najibabad [a town in the district about 45 km from Bijnor] Cooperative Federation Sugar Mill – you are its Chairman.' Harish slyly added that the last car was the only one with an air conditioner and was the one always used by my predecessor. Taken aback by this extravagant use of so many cars, and keen to project an impression of austerity at the outset, I barked out my first order as DM: 'I don't want a car with air conditioning and, in any case, why should the Najibabad car be kept here in Bijnor? Send it back.' There was a hushed silence and incredulous glances were exchanged between the gathered household staff, who were probably wondering if I was crazy to return the only car with an air conditioner, especially in the sweltering heat. 'I don't want to see this car here tomorrow morning,' I repeated and went inside the house. When I reported this incident over the phone in the evening to Indira, still in Delhi with the kids, she gave me kudos: 'Well done!' But she added, with a rueful chuckle, 'There goes my chance of being driven around in an air-conditioned car!'

Pro-Tip: As much as one may find it superficial, appearances matter. Whether it is a spartan lifestyle in the district or an ironed shirt worn to office, the image you paint in others' mind sticks.

So, I suffered the hot summer of 1992 taking long and sweaty drives around the district in my non-air-conditioned car, but the first impression I had created of living a spartan life had its impact. Word gets around quickly in a district where there are no secrets and everyone knows what everyone else does. To add to the spartan image, I let my staff and the local SDM and Tehsildars (revenue officials) know that on my weekly field visits, I expected only a simple aloo-puri meal, so they did not need to take the trouble and incur the expense of arranging the usual, extravagant 'all the trimmings' lunch for the visiting DM. It was important to spread the word around that the new DM was focused only on work and not interested in the trappings of the district office. It was also important for the lower-level field staff to know that the new DM was 'going walkabout', meeting local people to understand their problems first-hand and trying to find solutions.

Perceptions matter

Diwali is an important festival in the Hindu calendar, but it is even more important for testing a DM's character in UP. Ever since the time of the British Raj, this festival has been the occasion for local zamindars and traders to pay obeisance to the *mai-baap* of the district by making their way to the DM's residence with gifts. In the Indian Civil Services (ICS), as the IAS was known before Independence, officers were expected to strictly follow the *phal-phool* (fruits and flowers) rule. This meant that it was de rigueur to accept Diwali gifts from the locals that were edible or perishable, such as sweets, dried fruits or flowers, but it was a complete no-no to take valuable gifts such as precious metals or jewellery. This did not always mean, however, that the local zamindars followed the rule and so it was up to the DM to enforce the *phal-phool* rule.

I was determined to follow in the best Diwali traditions of my ICS predecessors and so, during the festival season in October 1992, took a simple precaution to deal with the endless stream of visitors bearing gifts. I asked my IAS Officer Trainee, Kamran Rizvi, who was on a year's district training stint in Bijnor, to be on duty with me at the DM's residence when the Diwali visitors came. While I received the visitors in my 'camp office' (home office), Kamran was positioned in the adjacent drawing room. As the visitor was offered a cup of tea and some sweets, his gift was taken inside by a helper and quickly examined by Kamran to confirm that its contents conformed to the *phal-phool* rule.

Everything went smoothly until a certain wealthy mill owner from Kiratpur came to offer his Diwali greetings. One of the richest men in the district, owning a number of rice and oil mills, he told me he had personally conveyed Diwali greetings to Bijnor DMs for over 50 years and that it was an honour to greet me as well. He handed over his gift, saying it was only a box of dried fruit. It was duly taken away to be examined by Kamran. As soon as the mill owner left my camp office, Kamran rushed in and asked me to follow him inside. The gift, a clearly expensive set of six solid silver goblets, was a blatant violation of the *phal-phool* rule. Using the intercom, I quickly called up the guard at the entrance of the residence's driveway and told him to stop the mill owner and request him to return to the house. The latter came back to my camp office and entered somewhat nervously. Keeping my calm, I returned his Diwali gift, saying diplomatically that there must have been some mistake, because his gift did not have any dried fruit and actually contained 'something else'. Sweating profusely, the mill owner apologized for the 'mistake' and vanished from sight. He had deliberately tested my integrity by violating the *phal-phool* principle but I had stuck to it. Word about this spread like lightning around the district.

To complement our efforts in the district to walk the straight and narrow path, Indira, now in Bijnor with the kids, made sure that our household was run on a strictly 'fully paid for' basis. This meant that, unlike many DMs' households in UP, we paid for all our requirements just as we had done in Delhi, whether it was food supplies or potato seeds for planting. It seemed that this was an unusual practice in Bijnor but we stuck to it and it added to the reputation for austerity of the new DM and his family.

Tackling development challenges

One of my first village visits was to the Chandpur subdivision, where I discovered that access to clean drinking water was a major problem. While providing piped water supply to all in these rural areas was going to take a lot of time and resources (in fact it was 27 years later, in 2019, that we received the approval of the Union Cabinet for the Jal Jeevan Mission – to provide piped water supply to every rural household in the country), even providing access to safe drinking water through handpumps was a big challenge, since in most of the cases, the existing handpumps were 'shallow'. These drew groundwater from a depth of only about 30–40 feet. Consequently, there was a high likelihood that the water from these shallow aquifers was contaminated. When some women in a village in the Chandpur subdivision told me that they fell sick after drinking water from the shallow handpumps, I asked the District Jal Nigam (Water Corporation) engineer to study the problem and come up with options to deal with it.

Based on the technical assessment of the Jal Nigam engineer, we found that the most practical solution was to provide deep bore handpumps, otherwise known as 'India Mark II' (IM-II) handpumps, which drew water from a deeper aquifer with uncontaminated water. I decided, therefore, to launch a large-scale programme across the district to provide drinking water through IM-II handpumps. Not unexpectedly, the budget for providing drinking water in the district was limited and asking the state government for extra funds for this purpose was unlikely to yield positive results. I needed to try something new.

Calling a meeting of all government department heads in the district, I asked each one of them to earmark some funds from their existing budgets towards a programme to drill deep boreholes and install IM-II handpumps in villages. This would be a time-bound programme in mission mode. There was some initial resistance but, with some friendly 'persuasion' using the authority of the DM, they came around. In the first phase, we managed to install about 1,000 IM-IIs at strategic locations such as primary health centres and block and tehsil headquarters. Each of the five sugar mills in the district also contributed their share of funds. This effort to 'dovetail' funds from multiple sources for hurdling the usual departmental budget caught the attention of the state's Chief Minister (CM), Kalyan Singh, who wrote me a letter of appreciation.

Handling the fallout of the Babri Masjid demolition

While the development work we initiated in the district occupied most of my time, the pivotal moments of my tenure as DM Bijnor came during the tense period in the aftermath of the demolition of the Babri Masjid at faraway Faizabad (now Ayodhya) on 6 December in 1992. With one of the highest Muslim populations in the state, Bijnor district has a history of Hindu–Muslim tension, which was exacerbated when the Babri mosque was demolished by a mob. Anticipating a potential law and order problem, R.P. Singh, the Superintendent of Police, and I had set up Hindu–Muslim Peace Committees in advance across the district and stationed police forces near sensitive sites such as mosques and temples. The Peace Committees consisted of influential members of both communities and their role included anticipating potential communal tension and, if it arose, stepping in to calm down the situation. As soon as word reached us that the Babri mosque had been demolished, the Peace Committees swung into action and, as a measure of abundant caution, I called in the Army from the Corps Headquarters at Meerut to stage flag marches in the district. These measures worked and, with some minor exceptions, we were able to maintain law and order in the district.

On a suggestion from B.B. Bakshi, the Additional Superintendent of Police and a veteran police officer, we created a team of carpenters and masons and put them on 24×7 emergency standby. Sure enough, during the night of 7 December 1992, a temple in Bijnor town was vandalized and its main door broken down. Our team of carpenters and masons swung into action and reconstructed the temple door overnight. The next day, we took the local Hindu–Muslim Peace Committee into confidence and put out the story in the media that it was this committee, with both Muslims and Hindus, which had paid for the reconstruction of the temple door. This news of an act of communal harmony spread like wildfire across the town and considerably lowered the prevailing tension.

Nothing like family to keep you on track

While the job of DM was extremely demanding, I found it was easier to retain one's sanity and keep to the straight and narrow path amidst all the chaos because of a good work–life balance, mainly due to my wife's efforts. Indira's career had borne the brunt of our shift from Delhi to Bijnor. To be with the family, she gave up a very good job as Assistant Editor at the *Economic Times* in Delhi and joined the Life Insurance Corporation (LIC) office in Bijnor, after being selected through a national competitive examination. This was only one of the many tough choices she made throughout her career in order to prioritize family over job. All of us, thanks to her, loved our time in Bijnor. Our daughter, Tara, was just four years old at the time and our son, Venkat, was one. Tara went to kindergarten in the local school and enjoyed exploring the grounds of the house and learned to play tennis with me on weekends. Venkat was starting to speak when we arrived in Bijnor and, to my wife's chagrin, the first word he uttered was not 'Amma' or 'Appa', but 'Mahendar', the name of his caretaker, who used to catch live rats from the garden and dangle them by the tail in front of an enraptured young Venkat.

We also used to escape to the nearby Jim Corbett National Park through Kalagarh in north Bijnor and take the boat down the Ramganga river to Dhikala in the heart of the wildlife park. The kids enjoyed hanging out with the hardworking elephants, on whose backs we wandered into the jungle, looking for tigers. On one memorable occasion at the Park, I ran into my old friend Brijendra Singh, a Corbett aficionado, and he suggested we take a helicopter ride over the reserve with the then visiting Union Minister for Forests and Environment, Kamal Nath. To my horror, I found it was not the helicopter pilot who was flying us but the Minister himself! Not very confident about the ability of a Minister to fly a helicopter, I looked apprehensively at Brij and hung on for dear life during the flight. Since I spent more time looking at the person flying the helicopter than at the wildlife below, I probably missed out on seeing a tiger, a very rare sight in the thick jungles of the reserve.

The family also looked out for opportunities to visit nearby Dehradun, the place of my first posting, when we could meet old friends, enjoy different kinds of food in a more cosmopolitan environment and also have our annual family photo shoot at the Circuit House with my friend Ajay Goyal, a professional photographer.

Apart from travelling, family time in Bijnor also included introducing young Tara to tennis, my favourite sport. Too small to hold a tennis racket in one hand, she got used to whacking the ball double-handed on both sides and showed great promise from day one. With a table-tennis table already installed on the second floor of the house, ping pong became another useful break from office work, and I remember some intensely competitive games played very late at night with Kamran, my young IAS officer trainee. One constant, however, despite the incredibly hectic job of a DM, was my regular 5 a.m. run.

Since Bijnor in 1992–93 was a district where a terrorist threat still continued due to the separatist Khalistan movement, a security detail would accompany me on my early morning run. It was a little disconcerting to have a Gypsy jeep with four police commandos armed with automatic rifles follow me when I ran on the highway towards Nehtaur, but I soon got used to it. My usual running routine consisted of 2 km one way and 2 km back. Inspired by my father, and having focused on fitness since my years of competitive tennis, I am convinced that my early morning running routine and passion for sports have injected extra energy into the way I have approached life throughout my career.

> **Pro-Tip:** Regular exercise is the formula for physical, mental and emotional well-being. One should always carve out at least 30 minutes for fitness during the day (or night).

The Total Literacy Campaign

Fortunately, many of my colleagues in Bijnor were also keen sportspersons and all that cumulative fitness-induced energy was required when we launched a very ambitious new development programme in the district: the Total Literacy Campaign (TLC). This was an adult literacy programme, aimed at women and girls between the ages of 15 and 35, whose literacy rates were well below 25 per cent. I had galvanized the entire district development machinery for this vital programme and we chalked out a strategy and road map to get the job done over a period of a year. As many as 6,00,000 women and girls across the district in the identified category were to be made literate. We needed 60,000 teachers for a teacher-student ratio of 1:10. Since women were best suited to teach a woman or a girl in these parts, we realized that the best instructors would be girls who had completed their class 12 and typically stayed at home for a couple of years before getting married.

As we started the programme, it became clear that it would not be easy to get the illiterate ladies to agree to be taught or to get the girls who had passed class 12 to come out and volunteer to teach. It did not help that the men of the household in a conservative rural district like Bijnor were strongly opposed to the idea of their womenfolk either being taught or teaching others. To overcome this hurdle, I got all my Tehsildars and Block Development Officers to meet with the gram pradhans (elected village heads, as they are called in UP) and encourage them to promote this very important campaign. I made several field trips and held meetings across the district with the local communities. We also enlisted the support of grassroots organizations and NGOs to promote the campaign. One of them was the Bharat Gyan Vikas Samiti, which had outstanding volunteers who performed street plays and skits to promote awareness about adult literacy. One of their favourite chants was '*Buniyad se, buniyad se, ka kha ga gha seekho, o mehnat karne wale*' (From the basics, from the basics, learn the alphabet, all you hard working people), which Tara picked up while joining me on my frequent literacy campaign trips, and would then recite at home.

While the TLC was slowly gathering steam, we were still struggling to get both trainees and teachers out in big numbers. Bijnor had a large Muslim population and a majority of both the trainees and teachers were Muslim. Then, a brilliant idea by Kamran Rizvi helped accelerate progress exponentially. He suggested I call a meeting of all the imams (Muslim priests) in Bijnor district and request them to use their authority to appeal to all the Muslim women and girls in their mosque's jurisdiction to come out and participate in the campaign.

It was the first time in the history of Bijnor district that the DM had convened such a meeting of over 200 imams. When I made the appeal, they all readily agreed and the next Friday, at the Jumma namaz (prayer), they made passionate appeals to their female community members to join the TLC for the good of their community. The appeal was effectively a fatwa, a religious edict, and it worked like magic. The very next day we had hordes of girls coming out to volunteer as teachers and even larger numbers of women and girls readily agreeing to be taught. This one action gave the programme a huge boost and we were well on our way to achieving the goal in the remaining six months of the campaign. As a bonus, the ongoing TLC campaign also helped in the healing of the communal wounds opened up by the Babri Masjid episode of 6 December 1992.

You can't please everyone

Towards the end of June 1992, I was called to the state headquarters in Lucknow to make a presentation on the Bijnor TLC, cited as a best practice, to the Chief Secretary and other senior officers. After the presentation, in a one-on-one meeting with the Chief Secretary, T.S.R. Subramanian, I was praised by him and told to continue the good work in Bijnor for at least another year. I returned to Bijnor that evening, full of confidence that we would now successfully complete the TLC and also take up other major development programmes.

I was naïve enough to think a pat on the back from the Chief Secretary would keep me in my job. Within a week of returning to Bijnor, on 2 July 1993, exactly one year since I had first arrived in that non-air conditioned DM's car, I was transferred out of the district and posted to Lucknow as Special Secretary, Agricultural Production Commissioner's branch. It turned out that a local politician, who was unhappy with me because I had confiscated his weapons for not repaying his excise dues, had met the Governor in Lucknow to have me removed from Bijnor, allegedly on the grounds that I was 'opposition-minded'. He must have made out a convincing case to the Governor, since I was transferred forthwith to Lucknow.

While I was very disappointed to leave the district at that point in time, there was not much else to do but to grin and bear the transfer. At least I had had the privilege of being the DM of Bijnor for exactly a year, and could leave with my head held high, having acquired a reputation, usually made or unmade early in one's career, of getting the job done, as well as that of personal integrity. We packed up our belongings into a small truck and left for Lucknow. Little did I realize that I was being launched into a critical phase of my career which would pay huge dividends going forward.

5

When it clicks, stay the course

STUMBLING INTO A SPECIALIZATION: THE SWAJAL STORY

IN MY EXPERIENCE, it is not always easy to discover one's true professional calling or passion, but that shouldn't stop you from working hard to find it. While I stumbled from job to job, and then from one sector to another after getting into the IAS, I sensed that sooner or later I would need to dive deep into a subject and be more than just a generalist. The closest I had come to specializing in a particular field was when I was in the Ministry of Textiles. It was finally in 1994, through the Swajal project, that the water and sanitation sector became my chosen field of specialization.

With my invaluable tenure as DM Bijnor coming to an abrupt end after only a year on the job, I took up my new job in Lucknow as Special Secretary, Agriculture Production Commissioner (APC) Branch, in early July 1993. With over 15 departments under its umbrella, the vast APC Branch was traditionally the dumping ground for recalcitrant officers

transferred from districts. Most officers posted here tried to
'escape' from the APC Branch to a 'better' department such as
Industries or to a corporation with *gadi-ghoda*, and were usually
successful in their efforts.

Not a little frustrated at having been unceremoniously
transferred from Bijnor, I called on J.L. Bajaj, the Agriculture
Production Commissioner, soon after joining at Lucknow.
'Which department do you want to work in?' he asked me, and
when I shrugged my shoulders to indicate no preference, he said,
'Go to Rural Development. The Secretary, K.R. Bhati, is very
good and you can learn a lot from him and the work they do
there.' And so I became Special Secretary, Rural Development.
Mr Bhati, an ex-Army officer, was indeed an excellent person
to work with and made me feel totally at home. However,
the work I was assigned – oversight of the rural employment
programme known as Jawahar Rozgar Yojana and the anti-
poverty, rural income-generating Integrated Rural Development
Programme – was not very stimulating. Having implemented
these programmes in the field in Bijnor, the idea of sitting at a
desk in Lucknow and monitoring their progress did not much
appeal to me.

What cannot be cured must be endured

While I did not start off in my new Secretariat job on an upbeat
note, I was fortunate to have a series of great bosses in quick
succession, first K.R. Bhati, then Rita Sharma followed by H.C.
Gupta and finally Atul Gupta. All of them kept a benevolent eye
on me from a distance and empowered me to act more or less
independently.

I was serving under H.C. Gupta when I was presented with
the opportunity of a lifetime. A World Bank team was visiting

Lucknow to discuss the preparation of a rural water supply and sanitation project, and my boss nominated me to be the focal point for engaging with them. The discussions with the World Bank team turned out to be fascinating, with the Task Team Leader, Xavier Legrain, introducing me to the water sector. In return, I introduced him to some high-risk driving in the Kumaon hills, when I was at the wheel of my Gypsy jeep. Sitting in front beside me, he clung to the glove compartment handle for dear life as we took the hairpin bends at high speed. He was also quite exhausted as we trekked up and down the hills, listening and talking to village communities to better appreciate their problems.

The birth of Swajal, and the start of my lifelong association with water and sanitation

Swajal was a World Bank-funded water supply and sanitation project in the UP hills and Bundelkhand, the two most water-scarce regions of the state. I created a Project Management Unit (PMU) to design and implement the project and set about putting together a core team to help me manage it. Given carte blanche by my boss, I handpicked the core members, starting out with one of the best officers from my Bijnor district team: J.P. Shukla. An excellent community mobilizer with the ability to think outside the box, he was an obvious choice to head our Community Development unit. Umesh Pathak, who worked as District Development Officer in Lucknow district, was hired to lead the Operations unit. I was very lucky to get J.K. Natu, an outstanding officer from the Finance and Accounts service, to manage our Finance unit. V.K. Verma, a top-class IIT Kanpur engineer from the Irrigation Department, was put in charge of our Monitoring and Evaluation unit, and

V.K. Agarwal, an experienced executive engineer from the UP Jal Nigam (water corporation), became the head of our Engineering unit. This small team of dedicated professionals proved to be the nucleus of the programme.

Pro-Tip: It is worth spending time and energy in creating the 'dream team'.

We hired office space just outside the Secretariat and began to function in a way that was very different from the slow and ponderous working of the Secretariat, where file-pushing was the norm. We spent hours brainstorming on project design and approach, determined to come up with unique and innovative approaches to the community-based service delivery of rural water supply and sanitation. During one of these intense sessions, it struck me that we should also have a unique name for the project to reflect its special design, and not just refer to it by its official, colourless World Bank title: 'UP Rural Water Supply and Environmental Sanitation Project'. We thus began hunting for the appropriate title and Umesh Pathak, our Operations unit head, came up with the perfect name: Swajal. In Hindi, Swajal means 'our water', signifying community ownership. The word also easily rolled off the tongue and was immediately accepted by everybody. It became the official name of the project. We also decided to have a symbol for the project, which was inspired by a little girl named Govindi from the hills of Pithoragarh. The Swajal symbol thus became a little girl with a ponytail, cupping her hand to drink water from a tap.

The Swajal Logo

The core Swajal team and I spent hours, both in Lucknow and in the project area – the Garhwal and Kumaon Himalayas, and Bundelkhand – trying to grasp the realities of designing a project that would enable rural communities in water-scarce areas to manage the service delivery of safe drinking water and sanitation. The NGOs, or Support Organizations, as we called them, brought all their hard-earned experience to bear and helped us with the project. Jointly, we designed the Swajal project to empower communities with the capacity to plan, implement and maintain their very own water supply and sanitation systems. The Swajal project thus became the first large-scale community-led water supply and sanitation project in India and its design and approach were emulated by many other states.

All it takes is one woman

Even as my team and I designed the Swajal project, we had to go through a formal process of obtaining approval of the state Cabinet before we could proceed with negotiations with the World Bank for a project loan of $60 million (approximately

Rs 450 crore). At that time, in 1996, Ms Mayawati was the CM of UP and, from what little I knew of her working, ran the state and her Cabinet in a firm manner. I was, therefore, a little apprehensive when my boss, Indrani Sen, suggested that I, the relatively junior Project Director, make the project proposal presentation to the Cabinet chaired by the CM. There was good reason to be nervous, since we were proposing to accept a key condition of the World Bank: sharing of the capital cost of the water supply schemes by the Swajal village communities, as well their taking full responsibility for the operation and maintenance.

Making the case to the Cabinet for villagers to pay for their water was not going to be easy. I prepared well for the Cabinet meeting but was more than a little nervous when I was called into the meeting room and made to sit at one end of the long conference table. At the other end sat Ms Mayawati, one of the only two women in the room; the other was Indrani Sen, seated behind me. The Cabinet Ministers were arrayed down the length of the table, seven on each side, all of them men. After I made my brief presentation, emphasizing the cost recovery element of the project design, each Minister was asked by the CM to state his opinion. The very first gentleman on my right shook his head vehemently and said, 'Madam, the project is fine but we cannot expect rural communities to contribute to the cost of a drinking water scheme. We will lose the next election if we do so.' As if on cue, all the other Ministers nodded in agreement, and I had the sinking feeling that the project proposal would surely be rejected.

The CM had said nothing until now but after the last Minister's rejection of the cost recovery principle, she finally spoke. To my utter surprise, she said, 'None of you understand the plight of women in our villages. They spend their whole life fetching water from long distances, while the men waste all the family's money on liquor and gambling. A small contribution by the community to the cost of the scheme is fine since piped water to the village will significantly reduce the drudgery of women and girls. Project approved.' I was very relieved and made a mental note of how the CM had stuck to her instincts and, disregarding the potential political fallout, taken a major policy decision to introduce an element of cost recovery in the rural water supply sector. This was the first instance in the country of cost sharing by the user community for a large-scale rural water supply and sanitation project, and it would have a major cascading effect in times to come. The Swajal project loan was signed with the World Bank in the middle of 1996.

From Swajal to Swajaldhara

Once the loan agreement with the World Bank was signed, project implementation began in earnest. For my team and me, this involved extensive travelling to the field and visiting village communities. I once took the then JS, Water and Sanitation, Government of India, Palat Mohandas, on one of these long treks to a Swajal village in the Garhwal Himalayas. He was so impressed by the way the village community, especially the women members of the Village Water and Sanitation Committee, was managing its own spring-fed and gravity-based water supply scheme that he decided to replicate and scale up the Swajal project in many districts across the country, and called the programme Swajaldhara (the stream or offshoot of Swajal).

As we started implementing Swajal, we realized that continual course correction of both project design and implementation process was the name of the game. The most practical suggestions on course correction came from the rural communities themselves. A good example of this was the reduction of the project scheme cycle of 27 months. We had initially thought that 12 months would be required for the village community to complete the planning phase. Instead, we soon found that the communities in the early phase of the Swajal project became impatient with what they saw as excessive planning and wanted the implementation phase to start earlier. Based on this feedback, we shortened the 12-month planning phase to three months and the overall scheme cycle from 27 months to 18 months. One of the early lessons I learned, therefore, was that a project design only holds good until the implementation commences, and that fancy 'five-star' models may look good on paper but do not always correspond to ground reality.

> **Pro-Tip:** The best can often be the enemy of the good. It is important to balance quality and implementability. Useful to follow the Goldilocks principle: not too much, not too little – make it just right.

Resisting temptation and staying the course

We lived in Lucknow for five years. While I continued working with enthusiasm and energy on the Swajal project and developed a deep interest in the water and sanitation sector, I was fortunate that the family loved the stay as well. The kids enjoyed attending the well-known Study Hall School and I resumed coaching Tara at tennis at the Civil Services Institute. Venkat, however, initially preferred playing golf at the friendly Lucknow Golf Course, primarily, I suspect, in order to sample the tasty sour fruit from the tamarind trees on the course. Meanwhile, I had been encouraging my incredibly smart wife who had planned to take the civil services exam before we got married, to do it now. And, despite having to face many more hurdles than I had in taking these exams – including juggling her latest job (at the National Bank for Agriculture and Rural Development in Lucknow) with managing two young kids as well as the household – Indira was successful in getting into the prestigious Indian Revenue Service (IRS). Accepting the IRS job meant she would need to spend almost a year away from the family to train at the National Academy for Direct Taxes in faraway Nagpur. She had almost made up her mind to decline this offer, but we jointly decided that taking up the IRS job would be an important career move for her.

With Indira in Nagpur, I had to take care of the kids for the duration of her nine-month training. Only now did I understand the challenges of balancing work with looking after young children, which Indira had seamlessly managed all along. I soon developed the habit of coming home from the office for lunch with the kids and then, before their afternoon nap in our one and only air-conditioned bedroom, bribing them into good behaviour with a packet each of the delicious sweet and sour candy called Fatafat. I usually had some Fatafat myself before vanishing from the room and going back to office. Not having too much confidence in my ability to look after the kids, Indira made frequent train trips from Nagpur to Lucknow in order to check up on what was happening and keep us all on our toes. For the kids and me, it was a great bonus to see her so frequently.

I was Project Director of Swajal for four years (1994–98). A year into my tenure, however, an attempt was made to transfer me elsewhere. I was summoned one day to Raj Bhawan to meet a senior IAS officer, the Secretary to the Governor. He came to the point straight away. Hinting that I must be fed up of working in a boring and low-profile sector like rural water supply, he asked me if I wanted to be reassigned to the important position of DM Varanasi. Since I did not appear to be duly impressed, he reminded me that Varanasi was one of the biggest and most prestigious districts in UP. Every young IAS officer in UP, the Secretary said, would give anything to be DM of one of the five fabled KAVAL (Kanpur, Allahabad, Varanasi, Agra and Lucknow) districts. 'This would also be a great opportunity to do another district after your Bijnor stint,' he said.

I thanked him for the offer and requested a day to think over it. Returning the next day, I told him I was very grateful for the consideration but would prefer to stay on as Director of the Swajal project, since I had spent only about a year on the job, was really enjoying it and would like to continue for at least a couple more years to properly implement it. Besides, my wife had just been posted to Lucknow as Assistant Commissioner, Income Tax, and we wanted to stay on in the city together for a while longer.

I had been very fortunate that Indira chose to move from job to job to accommodate my frequent transfers, but she was now settling into her new job in Lucknow and I too was coming into my own in the Swajal job. There was a great deal of satisfaction in designing and implementing a project to provide safe drinking water and sanitation to poor rural households and thereby transforming their lives, especially those of the women and girls who had to bear the brunt of fetching water over long distances. During my Swajal years, I decided this was my calling and was content about forgoing other 'prestigious' postings. I ended up continuing in the job for another three years, making it a total of four – a very long stint by UP standards.

Having decided that I wanted to continue specializing in water and sanitation and knowing I would not be able to continue much longer in the Swajal job after spending four years there, I applied for a position as a Senior Water and Sanitation Specialist in the World Bank's Water and Sanitation Program (WSP), located in Delhi. Based on my experience in the Swajal project, I was shortlisted for the job and put through a rigorous interview in Delhi by a panel of sector experts. A week later I received a call from Piers Cross, the Regional Team Leader of the WSP, who informed me that I had been selected for what he called the 'top job' – Country Team Leader of the WSP's India programme. I proceeded on secondment* from the IAS and joined the World Bank in Delhi on 15 April 1998. My persistence in staying the course with the Swajal project had paid off, after all.

Jack needs to master some trades too

While most young professionals in the private sector are, or become, specialists in a particular field (even if they tend to move from one organization to another), I am convinced that young IAS officers need to develop a specialization of their choice after they finish their field stint as DM. All IAS officers undoubtedly become specialists in general district administration. However, the system does not encourage post-DM job allocations to specific sectors based on the aptitude and interest of the officer. As a result, the officer tends to become a 'generalist' of sorts after the DM tenure, and could very well end up with postings in varied departments such as Finance, Home or Urban Development, without ever actually knowing much about these

---

* An IAS officer is permitted to proceed on secondment to an international organization, such as the World Bank, for a specified period, after which he has to return to the government.

sectors. Given that most IAS officers are involved with policy-making at a senior level, it is important to develop some level of expertise and experience of the sector to be truly effective. For this, a deeper dive into a particular sector at a relatively early stage of an IAS officer's career is critical. While I fortuitously became a 'water-and-sanitation-wala' through my Swajal experience, I think it is time that the system actively promotes specialization for young IAS officers and then posts them to the related sector.

OUTSIDER (1998–2016)

7 OCTOBER 2000

DEL ✗ IAD

AF 147-AF 26

INDIRA, TARA, VENKAT and I were at Delhi's international airport, this time checking in for Air France's flight to Washington DC via Paris. Each of us was allowed two pieces of luggage, so we checked in eight pieces in all. The kids were excited about the long flight ahead and thrilled to be served snacks and soda while settling into their comfortable business class (perks of being with the World Bank) seats. As the flight took off, they soon started watching their favourite Disney movies.

After spending a couple of years as the Country Team Leader of the WSP, I was excited to be relocating to the World Bank headquarters in Washington DC to work at a global level on water and sanitation. Across the aisle, Indira and I quietly discussed plans for a new life ahead of us in America. Having got used to our familiar and comfortable life in Delhi, we were apprehensive about the relocation to America, which we were sure would be a big change for all of us. 'Well, whatever else happens,' I finally said to Indira, who was by now half-asleep, 'the kids' tennis training should dramatically improve.'

The 20-hour journey, with a stopover in Paris, seemed unending at the time and we were all relieved and a little exhausted when the plane started its descent towards Dulles airport. Energized again, we unfastened our seatbelts and deplaned. We had a long wait at immigration and customs and then walked out of the airport into the pleasant fall sunshine. A long journey had ended and a new one was about to begin.

6

Knowledge, not authority, commands true respect

FROM A BUREAUCRAT TO A TECHNOCRAT

TRANSITIONING FROM ONE job to another is never easy, and it is even more complicated when the switch is from the work – and life – environment of a civil servant. As an IAS officer, one has plenty of subordinates executing one's instructions, but I was now relocating to a much more do-it-yourself job in an international organization, the World Bank. Here, my past credentials would not help me much, but the knowledge I had gained over the years would. And I would still have to earn the respect of my new colleagues. In retrospect, I had a soft landing, having spent my first two years with the World Bank (April 1998–October 2000) in Delhi itself. This had been my opportunity to transform myself from a jack of all trades into a water and sanitation 'master'. It was a steep learning curve.

'Foreign territory' at the World Bank in Delhi

When I joined the WSP in New Delhi in April 1998, I had some culture shocks. Like most IAS officers, I was used to our hierarchical governmental system, where juniors in your organization address you as 'sir'. Since I was the Director of the Swajal project, all my team members automatically called me 'sir'. In the WSP, however, even though I had been hired as the India Country Team Leader, I was quite taken aback on my first day on the job when a young lady team member welcomed me with a 'Hello Param, I'm Barbara.' Not too sure how to respond, I decided to follow that old adage of 'When in Rome, do as the Romans do', attempted a smile and said, 'Hi Barbara.' It took some getting used to, but I had no option except to shed my notions of self-importance and hierarchy, and get on mutual first-name terms with the team.

There were other work environment–related aspects I had to get used to as well. I did not mind so much the little cubicle of an office I was given, which was in sharp contrast to my large Director's room in the Swajal office in Lucknow. What took more time to get used to was that I had to sometimes fetch my own coffee from the machine. I was just growing accustomed to this 'heretical' practice when an IAS batchmate dropped by to say hello. He raised an eyebrow when he saw my little office, but his jaw dropped when he saw me slink out to fetch him a cup of coffee. 'You mean you have to get your coffee yourself?' he asked loudly, and I had to wave frantically at him to lower his voice.

Working in a flat hierarchy

As simple as it may sound, the most substantial adjustment I had to make was to learn to work solo and not depend on a host of subordinates to 'put up' draft notes to me for approval. In any case, I did not have many subordinates: we were a small team of only five water and sanitation professionals – each highly qualified in the sector. It was a new experience for me to try to lead through the power of knowledge and not from a position of authority.

I realized I had to build credibility within my own team to establish my water and sanitation credentials. My four years in the Swajal project came in handy since I was able to convincingly talk about the ground realities and challenges of water and sanitation service delivery in UP, one of the least developed states in India. In fact, the 18-month scheme cycle we had redesigned for Swajal became a great starting point for my team and me to exchange ideas on the merit of community ownership.

> **Pro-Tip:** There is no substitute for field or 'hands-on' experience. Go out there and do it yourself, preferably towards the beginning of your career.

It was time now to broaden my sector knowledge, including technical and policy aspects. This was especially important since the main mandate of the WSP was to provide policy, knowledge and capacity support to our major clients: the central and state governments of India. As the Country Team Leader, I was expected to lead this effort.

In the early days of my work in the WSP I was hesitant about engaging with our chief client: the JS in the Division of Drinking Water and Sanitation, Ministry of Rural Development. The JS, Palat Mohandas, was a senior IAS officer who had seen it all and heard it all. How was I, technically his 'subordinate' in the IAS, going to add any value to the WSP's technical assistance to the government?

Luckily for me, I had an ace up my sleeve. In my previous avatar as Project Director of Swajal, I had taken the same JS on a field visit to a remote village in the Garhwal Himalayas. Actually, it was more of a trek – 6 km steeply uphill and back – than a village visit. Mr Mohandas, though thoroughly exhausted after the trek, was very happy about the sheer achievement of completing it and became a firm fan of the Swajal project's community-led approach to water and sanitation delivery. While initially wary about interacting with me as WSP Country Team Leader, he soon warmed up to my new role and our effort to support the Government of India in designing and rolling out the Sector Reform Project or Swajaldhara. Palat Mohandas became such an enthusiastic supporter of the WSP and its invaluable services that he even signed an exclusive memorandum of understanding with us which we rather grandly labelled a Strategic Alliance. This gave the WSP a seat at the *sarkari* (government) table and much-needed clout vis-à-vis other development partners.

A knowledge-based world

I learned that knowledge was the real power in this game, but that it was not enough to just acquire knowledge; one also needed to learn how to deliver it to one's client, and then follow through to see that the client has effectively applied it on ground. Too often, when knowledge in a particular sector is exchanged, there is a gap between theory and practice, and this needed to be plugged.

The WSP, in the relatively safe space of Delhi and working with familiar clients, was the best place for me to educate myself about knowledge transfer and its application. The World Bank prides itself on being not just a 'money bank' but also a 'knowledge bank', and the WSP was one of its finest examples of a 'client-facing' programme that provided practical knowledge and policies, distilled from the best global practices, to its clients. I learned that there was an art to organizing 'participatory' workshops for our clients, which brought together government officials and NGOs from different states and sectors to share their experiences and lessons with each other. Some states then rolled out the lessons they had learned.

One of the most successful workshops we organized was the Cochin Rural Water and Sanitation Policy Workshop for state water Ministers in December 1999. It was a fascinating experience. We had senior politicians frankly exchanging views, in an informal setting, on the challenges and opportunities of scaling up water and sanitation service delivery. I can still visualize the then Gujarat Minister of Water Supply sitting on the floor of the conference room of the Taj Cochin hotel, earnestly talking about his state's attempts at sector reform. With a magnificent view of the ocean, the Taj Cochin was a great place to unwind and relax. Given the mellow mood all round, we managed to put out an impressively worded Cochin Declaration, duly signed off by all the participating Ministers, espousing the key principles of water sector reform. In following up with some of the states after the workshop, it was heartening to see that at least two of them, Andhra Pradesh (Chittoor district) and Kerala (Kasargod district), had started implementing some of the key principles of community service delivery endorsed at the Cochin workshop on the ground.

About a year or so into the new job, I began to enjoy my role as the leader of a knowledge and capacity transferring 'vehicle', quite a change from being mainly an implementer. It was also becoming fulfilling and fun working in a small team, each member with a different background but all working in a tight-knit manner with a common goal. It was a new experience as well to hire a few professionals from the 'open market', as opposed to having team members posted on deputation from other government departments. I selected the very bright Dr Satyajit Singh, an academic specializing in water, from Delhi University, to lead our policy work and the young and energetic Mike Webster, a South African water engineer, who quickly adapted to Indian conditions and became a valuable source of technical assistance to all our clients. By a strange coincidence, although we are five years apart from each other, the three of us share a birthday – 16 April – and continue to exchange birthday greetings on that date every year.

Cartoons can be serious business

A fringe benefit of working in the WSP was that we had a lot of fun in the office. One of my most enjoyable experiences was when we leveraged the knowledge of a technical expert in another field: the world of cartoons! It was the time of the year when the usual discussion ensued about the design of the calendar for the following year. It occurred to me that we should try something different for the millennium year of 2000, and I proposed that we bring out a cartoon calendar. The idea was that we would pick some important themes on water and sanitation and get an outstanding cartoonist to sketch out our ideas. Thus commenced the development of the first WSP cartoon calendar in late 1999. Deciding that only the best would do for us, we initially contacted R.K. Laxman, considered by many to be the top cartoonist in India. While Mr Laxman was too busy to take up our offer, he providentially suggested that we contact Sudhir Dar, also a highly rated cartoonist in the country. For us, Sudhir, who immediately accepted our offer, was *the* best, and thus began my 20-year association with him. It ended sadly in November 2019, when he passed away at the age of 88, just after completing the 2020 cartoon calendar – no longer from the WSP, but then a Swachh Bharat product.

The first WSP cartoon calendar we produced with Sudhir Dar for the year 2000 was one of the most fun experiences I had while working there. My team and I had several brainstorming sessions with Sudhir on the themes to be sketched and ended up with what I consider to be some of the best ones he ever did for us. Two of them stand out in memory. First, the one where the 'Great Indian Rope Trick' is being performed: a snake charmer playing his flute creating the mirage of a rope rising up like a snake. The tagline was: 'India achieves 100% drinking water coverage', while a horde of thirsty people around proclaimed its utter scarcity. The second was of an Indian holy man on the Varanasi ghats pouring out a jug of dirty-looking Ganga water for a disciple to drink and, seeing the reluctance on the latter's face, saying, 'It may be filthy but it is pure.'

Many years later, in 2017, Sudhir and I picked up from where we had left off when, as Secretary at the Ministry of Drinking Water and Sanitation, I requested him to sketch a Swachh Bharat cartoon calendar for us. His cartoons were big hits and he ended up doing three more sets for us in 2018, 2019 and 2020. His last cartoon, and certainly one of his best, completed in November 2019, was of PM Narendra Modi addressing the nation from the Red Fort during his first Independence Day speech (refer to the cartoon in the photo section), declaring an end to open defecation in the country, with the 'VIPs' shocked at such a base topic being mentioned on such an important occasion, while some 'ordinary' women were thrilled about it.

We went through several iterations to try to get the PM's face just right. One day, Sudhir would sketch an angry-looking PM and I would reject it. Another day there would be a timid-looking PM, and I would reject that too. The third time was a plump-looking PM and, yes, I rejected that too. When we finally arrived at the 'just right' PM, I remember Mrs Dar's words to her husband: 'This Param Iyer guy really drives a hard bargain, but you've got to admit it, the result is worth it.' In fact, the result was so good that Indira and I presented the original cartoon sketch to PM Modi at our farewell meeting with him on 20 August 2020.

While I was learning the ropes at the WSP in Delhi, my family was revelling in their action-packed life there. Indira, transferred from Lucknow to Delhi, had taken on a quasi-legal role as the Departmental Representative at the Income Tax Appellate Tribunal. This job gave her the flexibility to continue to keep a close eye on the kids' school and tennis activities. We chose to live in a rented apartment in Vasant Enclave in south Delhi, primarily because the Cosmic Tennis Academy, where Tara and Venkat were training, was only a 10-minute walk away. Both of them had started excelling in the sport and were winning state- and even national-level tennis tournaments in their age groups. While they regularly visited my father in Chennai and practised at the Krishnan Tennis Academy – which he managed along with the Krishnans, India's great tennis family – it soon became apparent that their tennis training would need to be ramped up if they were to enter the big league and compete internationally. Such training facilities were not available in India at the time.

Continental shift – relocating to Washington DC

In mid-2000, after spending a couple of years in Delhi, and just when we were wondering how to step up the quality of the kids' tennis training, the perfect opportunity presented itself: I was asked if I wanted to relocate to Washington DC, to the World Bank headquarters, to coordinate the WSP's global knowledge and learning programme for rural water supply and sanitation. Apart from being a recognition of the knowledge and policy work my team and I had done in WSP India over the previous two years, the shift to Washington DC was a chance to broaden my knowledge and experience to a global level. Indira, who had once obtained a scholarship to do a PhD in economics at a top US university but not pursued it, now took study leave from the IRS to follow her earlier plan. From the children's perspective, it was exciting to travel and live abroad and, needless to say, for the family as a whole, it was a great time to step up Tara and Venkat's tennis training to international standards and give them the best possible opportunity to make tennis a career.

We relocated to Washington DC in the first week of October 2000 and were met at Dulles airport by a friend who was working in the World Bank as an energy specialist. He packed us and our eight suitcases into his Grand Caravan minivan and drove us to his home in McLean, Virginia, where his wife had a sumptuous south Indian meal – rice, sambar and beans curry – ready for us. We stayed at a nearby apartment complex for the first couple of weeks while looking for a house to rent. The decision to take a house on Beverly Avenue in McLean was made, like in the past, primarily because it was the closest residential area to one of the top tennis academies in the Washington DC area – the Four-Star Tennis Academy – run by their veteran head coach Bob Pass. The academy was still about 10 miles (16 km) from our house, and Indira, used to driving our little Maruti 800 at slow speeds in Delhi, had to quickly get used to driving the kids there in our new, huge Toyota Sienna minivan at high speeds on the I-495 interstate. For their part, Tara and Venkat soon adapted to the intense physical conditioning which, relatively neglected back in Delhi, was essential for a tennis player intending to compete internationally.

In the meantime, I was getting used to the workplace at the World Bank headquarters. It was a fascinating, multinational, multi-cultural environment, with cuisines from at least 20 countries on offer daily at the superb staff cafeteria in the main complex building.

My primary responsibility as a Senior Water and Sanitation Specialist was to act as the global rural water and sanitation knowledge coordinator of the WSP, and work with the 150 professionals located in 20 countries around the world. Each one of those country teams was working with its government and other clients to support them in developing policies and practices in the water and sanitation sector, ultimately to help their poorest citizens gain access to water and sanitation services. My job was to connect the WSP's country offices through the exchange of lessons and experiences, and develop some key 'knowledge products' which would support our country teams in providing relevant global lessons and technical assistance to their country clients.

I plunged into work, coordinating with colleagues working across different regions of the World Bank, and was soon appointed the co-Chair of the Rural Water and Sanitation Thematic Group (RSWTG) of the Bank. The other co-Chair, Jennifer Sara, an outstanding water and sanitation professional then working in the World Bank's Africa region, had already made a name for herself for her knowledge and experience in the rural water and sanitation sector.

Within a few months of my joining in DC, Jennifer and I, along with Val Curtis of the London School of Hygiene and Tropical Medicine, developed a major global knowledge programme we called the Public–Private Partnership for Handwashing with Soap (PPP-HWS). We learned from Val and her team that the simple act of washing one's hands with soap could save the lives of more than a million children a year. In the year 2000, this was quite a radical idea but it has subsequently not only been proven to be true but also widely accepted – and became one of the most effective defence mechanisms against the coronavirus during the global pandemic of 2020. In late 2000, however, it was a challenge to bring together key global stakeholders to promote the mundane practice of handwashing with soap with a public health objective. So, as part of the World Bank's RWSTG learning agenda, Jennifer, Val and I created a public–private partnership bringing together the biggest soap companies in the world, health experts and top global agencies in a coalition aimed at securing and promoting global knowledge about the important health benefits of handwashing with soap. We also planned to curate and integrate this knowledge into some country implementation strategies.

Knowing is not necessarily understanding

The PPP-HWS included the three biggest soap companies in the world (Unilever, Procter & Gamble and Colgate-Palmolive), the two top public health research groups (the London School of Health and Tropical Medicine and the Centers for Disease Control, Atlanta), and the major international development agencies (UNICEF, USAID and the World Bank). Three developing countries agreed to implement the knowledge and research coming out of this partnership: India (through the state of Kerala), Ghana and Peru. The World Bank provided the secretariat for this partnership. In many ways, the PPP-HWS was a win–win for all the stakeholders: the private sector soap companies saw this as an opportunity to sell more soap, while the research organizations, development agencies and participating countries saw it as a way to promote and improve public health.

While we were convinced of the benefits of and need for handwashing with soap, out of the three countries which were the early implementers, ironically, India – which I was personally supporting – turned out to be a failure. Despite the huge effort, Val Curtis, Yuri Jain (Unilever India) and I made in working with the Kerala government to develop their PPP-HWS plan, and just when the programme was all set to commence in late 2002, the state government decided to scrap it. The reason given to me was that the state's political leadership felt this was a World Bank/capitalist (multinational soap company) ploy to undermine the socialist traditions of the state. I learned something very important from this failure: while we had the support of the top civil servants in Kerala for the PPP-HWS programme, I had not engaged with the political leadership, assuming they would follow the advice of their bureaucrats. But they didn't. This lesson would stand me in good stead when we embarked on the Swachh Bharat Mission many years later because, good intentions apart, political leadership is a golden ticket to implementing big ideas.

Knowledge exchange in Afghanistan

As part of my 'knowledge' work in the World Bank, I had made a trip to Kabul, some months after the US invasion of Afghanistan following the 9/11 attack. Since there were no commercial flights to Kabul at that time, I had to board a special UN chartered flight from Dubai to Kabul. The aircraft had to make a unique, security-related diving manoeuvre while landing at the heavily fortified Kabul airport, which was quite an experience. To complete the 'wartime' feel, I was whisked into an armoured car and driven to the heavily fortified guest house run by the World Bank.

Our client, the Government of Afghanistan, was keen to develop a National Solidarity Programme in their war-torn country and strengthen local governance through small infrastructure projects. Using my Swajal experience, I was to design and develop the process whereby the *jirga*s (local councils) would apply to the government for block grants. It took me two hard weeks of travelling to the field in the heavily land-mined countryside and engaging with the local tribal councils to understand what their needs and demands really were. During this fascinating period, I travelled to the Panjshir valley, saw many blown-out Soviet tanks littering the roadside, and visited the mausoleum of the iconic Ahmed Shah Masood, former top commander of the Northern Alliance, who was assassinated two days before 9/11. One of the highlights of my visit was witnessing the unique sport of Buzkashi, a sort of horseback polo, except that instead of playing with a mallet and ball, these gifted horsemen used the carcass of a calf to score a goal. Apparently, this was the only sport the Taliban had allowed to be played during its regime.

Becoming a China watcher

As Global Rural Coordinator in the WSP, my knowledge work also included researching and authoring some analytical pieces related to the water and sanitation sector, which had policy implications for our clients: the countries which borrowed from the World Bank. In stark contrast to the rap on the knuckles I had got in Lucknow for writing an op-ed analysing the Environment (Protection) Act of 1986, I soon learned that to progress in the World Bank, it was important to author a few quality 'knowledge products' to really establish myself as a global water and sanitation guru.

> **Pro-Tip:** If you want to rise in your career or organization, understand the outcomes that are valued and direct your efforts accordingly.

During 2001–05, I immersed myself in the World Bank's China programme and made several trips to the country. My initial exposure to China was an experience. In late 2002, I had flown to Kunming, capital of Yunnan province in southwestern China, to study their rural water utility model, and was invited to attend a formal banquet in a local hotel the same evening. I was put at the circular head table with the host sitting opposite me. I had been warned in advance that in China, the host, usually a senior party or government official, would offer an alcoholic toast to the guest of honour, myself in this case, and I was expected to respond by toasting him back. Since I am a lifelong teetotaller, I thought I would be excused from the ritual but the host insisted on filling my glass with Baijiu, the premier whisky of China, and raised a toast to me. On the spur of the moment, I turned to one of my team members, a Malaysian-Chinese professional water engineer called Eddie Hum, and suggested that he raise the toast as my proxy. The host was not too amused but agreed to toast with Eddie. The latter soon became my 'designated drinker' in formal banquets. Irrespective of how much he drank 'in the line of duty', Eddie, a PhD in engineering from the Asian Institute of Technology, Bangkok, and a thorough professional, was always on time for work the next morning and provided outstanding technical assistance to me for all my work in China.

After travelling extensively in China, especially to the provinces of Yunnan, Gansu, Shaanxi and Sichuan, I learned that the provincial government offered very few subsidies in the water and sanitation sector, even in the less affluent rural areas, and households were treated as consumers, with water tariffs set for providing tap water in their homes. In India, in comparison, drinking water, piped or otherwise, was almost always provided free to rural households (the Swajal project being a small but significant exception). I also found that in China, the rural water utilities ran relatively efficiently because the incentives were well designed. Water tariffs were set by the County Price Bureau, and the water utility manager had to collect a minimum percentage of the water dues; otherwise his salary was cut. Households, even the poorer ones, were willing to pay the water fees as long as they were provided with good service in terms of quantity and quality of water.

Relating the China model to my experience in India, where traditionally policymakers are reluctant to charge for drinking water, I wrote a piece on China's rural water supply model titled 'Willingness to pay and willingness to charge', which was widely shared in other countries. The key policy implication of this knowledge product was that rural households, even the poor ones, were willing to pay an affordable fee for good service delivery, since they bore heavier coping costs, such as the time spent on fetching water, when this was not available.

I later co-authored another piece, along with Professor Jennifer Davis of Stanford University, on two of the key challenges facing the water and sanitation sector globally: sustainability and scale. Many pilots and small projects had successfully demonstrated effective models of rural water supply service delivery, but very few of them had succeeded in going to scale. Jennifer Davis and I researched many rural water supply systems around the world and produced a piece titled 'Taking sustainable rural water supply services to scale: where are the bottlenecks?', which addressed these two core issues. Both these knowledge products were widely appreciated in the World Bank's water and sanitation circles and further cemented my reputation as an international expert in the sector.

Initially starting out in an alien environment, my first eight years in the World Bank, 1998–2006, taught me many things, including enhancing my sector expertise, enabling me to work independently without a paraphernalia of subordinates, and learning how to become a true sector professional and command respect on the strength of one's knowledge.

7

Take a break if you need to, it's OK

ROAD MANAGER TO A PROFESSIONAL TENNIS PLAYER

IN EARLY 2006, after we had lived and worked in Washington DC for more than five years, a tipping point arrived in the form of a key family decision. Tara, having played international junior tennis at the highest level, had achieved a world ranking of no. 42 in the International Tennis Federation (ITF) junior rankings. Now, after spending a year on a full tennis scholarship at Duke University, Durham, North Carolina, she was ready to move up to the next level and compete professionally. She was passionate about tennis and loved nothing more. It was her life and her dream to be one of the best players in the world. If ever there was a time for her to take the plunge and enter the big league, this was it. But she needed a road manager cum coach to accompany her on the women's tour, and I was the person best qualified for that role.

Having nurtured Tara's tennis career from the start, I was excited at the prospect of accompanying her at this crucial stage of her tennis journey, even though it meant leaving the World Bank. There comes a time in all of our lives when we need to assess what matters most to us and to our loved ones, to put career second and family first. Indira had been doing it for many years and it was now my turn. The choice for me was clear. The bonus was that this was a job I had dreamt about ever since Tara hit her first tennis ball in Bijnor many years ago. It was now becoming a reality.

Hitting the road

Putting my career in the water and sanitation sector on hold, I resigned from the World Bank on 11 April 2006 to take up my new role as road manager to Tara Iyer, professional tennis player.

Given that it would have been prohibitively expensive for us to continue to live in Washington DC without a World Bank salary, we decided to relocate to Delhi later that year and make it Tara's tennis training base.

Over the next two years, Tara and I travelled to more than 20 countries across five continents, with Tara playing in more than 40 professional tournaments. During this period, as road manager, I performed the following roles: (i) coach, (ii) dad, (iii) itinerary planner, (iv) booker of budget airline tickets and low-cost hotels, (v) washer of tennis clothes and drier of soaking tennis shoes, (vi) recorder of tennis match statistics and, well, (viii) doer of all other 'odd jobs'. The only task I was not in charge of while on the tour (luckily for Tara) was preparing meals. We usually had breakfast at the hotel restaurant, lunch at the tournament venue, and the evening meal was in the hands of 'chef' Tara. She enjoyed coming up with healthy yet tasty food, and was in charge of whipping up our simple dinner, typically consisting of tuna sandwiches, microwaved vegetables and boiled chickpeas. There were times, of course, when we would throw the healthy diet to the winds, and binge on junk food like McDonald's burgers and French fries or an occasional pizza – all global products and available even in the remotest of towns in most countries.

Before I plunged into my job as road manager, Indira and I had decided it might be useful for me to pilot this new role with our son Venkat as the guinea pig! Venkat, just 15 then, was also showing great promise as a tennis player. A gifted athlete, he was ranked no. 1 in his age group in the Mid Atlantic Tennis Association region, had just been selected to play the Junior Davis Cup for India, and rapidly rose to the rank of no. 115 in the ITF under-18 rankings – no mean feat in a very competitive sport. (Venkat, too, went on to play professional tennis eventually. Recurrent injuries, however, would curtail his run on the men's tour, but more on that later.)

So, in May 2006, shortly after resigning from the World Bank, I took Venkat to Turkey to play his first ITF under-18 junior tournaments. This was the big league for young Venkat and the two back-to-back tournaments in Istanbul were a great experience for him, and me. While Venkat achieved a major milestone by earning his first ITF points in the second tournament, reaching the quarter-finals, I picked up valuable tips from a road manager's perspective. As a fringe benefit, we also greatly enjoyed Turkish cuisine, especially the famous doner kebabs.

My road manager's notes from the Istanbul trip highlighted some insightful tips while helping me frame my metrics to assess Venkat's, and then Tara's, form. For Venkat, it was going to be important to improve his overall fitness and, in particular, his strength. On a more technical front, he had to hone the forehand into a big weapon and provide more depth to his second serves. He also asked me to monitor the percentage of first serves he made successfully as well as the number of double faults. I thus learned from the road manager pilot to take notes and track match statistics during each match, and also to be more patient when Venkat made too many unforced errors. These were all useful tips which came in handy for my upcoming role as road manager to Tara.

A steep learning curve

After Venkat and I returned from Istanbul to Washington DC, I joined the children's tennis coach, Vesa Ponkka, for a week of intense coaching for Tara, prior to her setting out for her first series of tournaments in India. Vesa, a soft-spoken Finn who had coached Tara and Venkat for the past five years at the Junior Tennis Champions Center, had played professional tennis himself and knew a thing or two about playing on the tour. He advised us to set realistic goals for Tara, not to be disappointed by early losses, and to make sure she got plenty of rest and practice after playing two or three tournaments in a row.

One of Vesa's key principles was to maintain a level 'coaching' field for all his trainees. He would devote more time to those who put in greater effort, and spend correspondingly less time with those who did not make a 100 per cent effort. With Tara's strong work ethic, Vesa ended up spending a great deal of time coaching her, and then, just before she was embarking on a professional tennis career, he spent even more time that week to prepare her for the road ahead.

Tennis Stats for Venkat Iyer

Tournament/match: ITF Istanbul
Date: 23-6-2006
Name of opponent: Pavel Liska
Surface: Hard
Final match score: 6-3 4-6 6-2   Set # 1   Set score: 6-3

	1	2	3	4	5	6	7	8	9	10	11	12	Tot
Server's initials	V	L	V	L	V	L	V	L	V				
1st Serve Down the mid-M / Wide-W / Body-B	M W M		W B M		W M M W		W M		W M W				
2nd Serve / **Double Faults**	X X		X		X		X X		X				
Return of Return Errors (F or B)	Fx		Bx		Fx		Fx		Bx				
Return of Serve (winners/errors)		✓ X		X X		✓ ✓		✓ ✓					
Forehand Winners (X-Court, DTL)	XC XC	X X	XC DTL		XC XC	DTL	XC	XC DTL	XC DTL				
U/F Errors:	X		X	X X	X	X	X X	X					
Backhand Winners (X-Court, DTL, Inside Out)	DTL X✓		DTL X✓	XC	DTL X✓	DTL	XC	DTL	DTL				
U/F Errors:	X	X X	X	X X	X	X	X X	✓	X				
Net Moves	✓✓		✓		✓✓	✓	✓	✓✓	✓				
Winner's initials	V	L	V	L	V	V	L	V	V				

Comments for set: Good serving. 2nd serve needs more depth. V needs to step in more for forehand. Great net moves. Useful to pull out first set!

Road Manager's Stats Sheet, 2006

Pro-Tip: Treat everyone fairly, but not equally.
Different people bring different skills and effort to
the table.

We travelled to Delhi in June 2006 and Tara won her first
match in an ITF women's tournament in the capital against a
girl from China but lost in the next round to an Indian rival. We
trained in the heat of Delhi for another week or so before leaving
for China in early July to play three ITF tournaments in a row.

I was visiting China again, but now in a very different
capacity. It was Tara's first visit to the country and her first
tournament was in the city of Chongqing, in southwestern
China. This was a $25,000 ITF tournament and since Tara did
not have enough ITF points to earn entry directly into the main
draw, she had to play in the qualifying rounds. It was hot – well
above 100°F (38°C), Chongqing being known as one of the four
'furnace' cities in China – and Tara literally sweated her way
through the first three qualifying rounds, winning tough matches
against Chinese opponents. In fact, after winning her third and
final qualifying match, her tennis shoes got so wet that I had to
blow-dry them at night with the hairdryer in the hotel room to
get them ready before her big match, the first round of the main
draw. She was playing Shuai Chang, the top seed and a talented
Chinese player, who later went on to become a world no. 17.
Overawed by the occasion, Tara lost in straight sets, making too
many unforced errors off her forehand and not getting a high
enough percentage of first serves. I had taken copious notes of
the match and, later, we analysed the data to understand what
had worked and what hadn't.

Tara played two more tournaments in China, in the cities of Chengdu and Changsha, and did reasonably well in both, winning two qualifying rounds in the second tournament and three in the third tournament. It was not quite the dream start to her professional career we had hoped for, and we realized it was going to be a steep learning curve, both for Tara as a player and for me as a road manager.

One of the critical lessons Tara learned from the China trip was the need for a stronger defence from the back court, especially when her big weapons – forehand and serve – were not clicking. Second, she needed to hit better angles, outside the 'box' and, third, it was important for her to use more topspin on the forehand to prevent the ball from sailing out. The most practical tip the road manager learned, from the China visit, however, was to carry at least three pairs of tennis shoes on the next trip!

We enjoyed ourselves thoroughly in China, with Tara getting used to the local food, especially the tofu soup and chicken chowmein, learning how to use chopsticks, and even picking up some basic Mandarin. The icing on the cake was a visit to the famous Silk Market in Beijing where, after some strenuous bargaining, we ended up with many more souvenirs than we had planned to buy.

However, returning to Delhi, where Indira and Venkat were also based now, was a relief, partly because we could go back to a regular training regimen, including intensive fitness, but also because we could enjoy home-cooked food again. And, as a bonus, I did not have to wash tennis clothes for a while! While Tara took a break after the demanding China trip, I caught up with Venkat's training, which was progressing at the Siri Fort Sports Complex under the watchful eye of Aditya Sachdeva, one of India's best tennis coaches. Tara soon got back to a regular practice and fitness routine, but one worry was the niggling injury she had developed in her left knee some time back during an intense training session, which flared up occasionally. She regularly applied ice to the kneecap after training and after matches, but the injury would clearly bear watching.

Treating triumph and disaster just the same

We set out for Nigeria in October 2006 to play two ITF tournaments there, to be followed by a third in Turkey before returning to Delhi. It was an experience for us to land at the dimly lit Lagos airport, and then take a rickety taxi along dark streets to our hotel, the rather grandly named Mainland Hotel. Its surroundings were grim, a bustling highway running behind it and signs of urban poverty all around. Along with all the other players, we were driven the next morning in a bus to the tournament venue, the Lagos Lawn Tennis Club. The lunch at the club was good: chicken stew and rice with the local 'porridge', a cassava paste dish. Tara had a good practice hit there with Montinee Thanphong, a fellow player from Thailand.

Having a few ranking points under her belt, Tara earned a place in the main draw and played well to beat a Nigerian girl in straight sets: 6–1, 7–5. Her next match, scheduled the following day, got rained out and we had to spend the whole day at the tennis courts, waiting for the courts to dry up. This involved another aspect of road manager duty: keeping the tennis player mentally focused and engaged during match delays. We typically did one of two things to keep Tara mentally fresh during match delays: she either read a book or listened to her favourite music to switch off. In this particular case, she preferred reading a book and was soon engrossed in an old classic – Dickens' *A Tale of Two Cities*.

When the rain finally stopped, Tara played her match against the second seed, a Slovenian named Zuzana Kucova. It was a fiercely competitive match with coaches on both sides cheering their players on from the stands. There were some nail-biting moments as Tara recovered from multiple breakpoints on her serve early in the second set by hitting her way out of trouble with some big serves and aggressive forehand winners. I was tense and even remonstrated with the chair umpire when he made an incorrect line call against Tara. Unfortunately, Tara lost narrowly: 6–7, 4–7. As she came off the court, fighting back tears, I gave her a hug and a pat on the back, realizing that words of consolation were not much use at such moments. Losing always hurts and I had to be her dad then, not coach.

The Nigeria trip reinforced a valuable lesson for Tara: going on the offensive and deploying her big weapons, serve and forehand, during tight situations in a match was the most effective strategy. Meanwhile, I had to learn to always keep cool and calm during the match, even in the most nerve-wracking moments, because if the coach looks tense, the player senses it and it affects her game. It took a few matches, but I finally mastered the art of appearing calm and composed during Tara's matches. This ability to appear calm in tense situations would pay rich dividends in all my future jobs as well.

We flew to Istanbul after the Nigeria trip. What I remember most clearly from this trip was not the tennis, though. On the second day of our stay there, I, by now an 'experienced' road manager, had my wallet – containing over $2,000 plus my credit card and driver's license – pickpocketed in a crowded minibus. It was a big shock to be suddenly penniless in a foreign country. I went to the local police station and made a formal complaint but, needless to say, it was of little use. Indira sent me some money through Western Union and I cancelled my credit card. Learning from this episode, I made it a point never to carry so much cash with me while travelling as a road manager. I have to confess, though, that while I did not have much cash on me then, I managed to be pickpocketed once again 12 years later, in Greece this time.

Back on the tennis front, Lagos and Istanbul proved to be a useful round of tournaments for Tara, worth 10 ITF points, bringing up her world ranking to the 500s but, more importantly, adding experience and the confidence that she could play with the best of them. Her forehand and serve were getting better and better but her backhand down the line needed more work. She was becoming mentally tougher as well, and handling the losses and the wins more effectively.

Back in India, Tara played a series of tournaments in different cities, including in Ahmedabad, where we visited the Sabarmati Ashram for the first time. There was a calm and sense of peace about the place which both of us could feel. We also travelled to Nottingham, England, where the cold and rainy weather were dampeners, both literally and figuratively!

We had now spent about a year on the tour and while the results were coming gradually, Tara's on-and-off knee injury was limiting the aggressive physical fitness training she required, essential for the strength and stamina to compete at the highest level.

Looking back at that first year on the tour, I remembered Vesa's advice about setting realistic expectations in the early stages. He had also been quite clear that the results would take some time to come. Despite being armed with his advice, the world of professional tennis was daunting for us, especially in the beginning. It was a dog-eat-dog world, with every player equally determined to beat the other and climb up the rankings. Having been used to winning most of her matches while playing as a junior, it took Tara some time to get used to the more frequent losses at the professional level. It was a while before I too came to grips with a core aspect of the road manager's job: boosting your player's confidence and keeping her motivated. Luckily, thanks to Vesa's training, both Venkat and Tara were used to recovering quickly after losing, but it still hurt, particularly if it was a closely fought match.

One of the closest matches Tara lost was a quarter-final in Indonesia. She lost 6–7 in the third set after squandering a match point in her favour and, furious with herself, flung her racket on the ground in disgust – and the frame cracked. This was the only time I had seen her lose her cool in such a manner. It was too sensitive a moment for me to chide her for such behaviour and she was back to her usual cheerful self after about an hour. I learned an important lesson from this episode: leave Tara alone for about an hour or so after a loss, let her cool down, both physically and mentally – and only then discuss match tactics and statistics, and what had gone right or wrong. In addition to match tactics, the main point I would always try to emphasize was that one learned more from a loss than from a win, and that there would always be another opportunity to win, since the next tournament was usually only a Monday away.

Pro-Tip: The timing of feedback is even more important than the feedback itself. Feedback is usually most effective when it is received in a calm frame of mind.

The hot streak

And so Tara and I started getting used to dealing with the lows and highs of the tour. A proud moment occurred when she was selected for India's Federation Cup team and travelled with the national team to Christchurch, New Zealand, along with Shikha Oberoi, Sunitha Rao and Ankita Bhambri. After that we went on two back-to-back trips to Japan and Indonesia where she earned some valuable ITF points. She had a great run at the Asian Tennis Championships in Tashkent, where she reached the finals, losing to Uzbek Iroda Tulyaganova.

All the hard work paid off during a glorious spell in the late summer of 2007, after about 15 months on the tour, when Tara won four ITF tournaments on the trot, two in Europe and two in India. Indira accompanied her for the European tournaments, as I was focusing on Venkat's training in Delhi during this period. Tara's first ITF tournament win came at Estoril, Portugal, in July 2007 and was followed up with another tournament win at Wrexham, UK. The breakthrough, however, came at home in India, when she won two ITF tournaments, back-to-back in Noida and Delhi, gaining the ultimate revenge when she beat Ankita Bhambri, a long-standing rival, in three very close sets in the Noida finals in front of a huge audience. My father, the now retired Air Marshal Iyer – who had managed the Krishnan Tennis Academy in Chennai for five years and also accompanied Tara and Venkat to many tennis tournaments, especially during their junior days – was present during the Noida finals. He always enjoyed reading about Tara's and Venkat's victories in the newspapers and was excited to see her win reported 'in ink' in *The Hindu* the next day. My mother, herself a tennis champion from her college days, was also present at this historic event. The week after, Tara won her fourth ITF tournament in a row at the Delhi Lawn Tennis Association stadium in Delhi. All the hard work was finally paying off.

Catching up with Venkat

While Tara was going up in the Women's Tennis Association (WTA) rankings, Venkat was also making rapid progress on the ITF junior circuit. He reached the semi-finals of a big junior ITF tournament in Delhi, winning matches against older and more experienced players, and was selected for the elite Mahesh Bhupathi Tennis Academy in Bangalore. The only problem was that, like Tara, he was susceptible to injuries, ranging from an elbow injury to a dull but recurring pain in the lower abdominal region, which restricted his ability to serve strongly, especially critical in the boy's game. However, blessed with lightning-fast reflexes and foot speed, Venkat had literally started making great 'strides' when he got injured again during a tournament in Rabat, Morocco, and had to pull out of the next tournament at Casablanca.

A safety net helps to take a tough decision

Tara was now rising rapidly in the WTA rankings, having reached no. 350 in the world and showing the potential to rise further. She became the top women's player in India after Sania Mirza. Along with the rise in rankings, unfortunately, there was also the increasing frequency in the flare-up of her left knee injury. It came to a head during a match in Trivandrum in late 2007, where she was playing superbly on the red clay but, for the first time in her tennis career, had to pull out of a match in the third set due to unbearable pain in the knee.

Returning to Delhi, Indira and I took Tara to a top sports doctor in Delhi to properly diagnose her injury. After a second consultation, we learned that Tara needed to have surgery for what was known as a lateral release of a tight tendon which was tugging and tilting her left patella (knee cap) outward. Serendipitously, Tara's tennis coach at Duke University in the US had been entreating Tara to come back and play tennis for Duke, since she was his best hope for winning a national title. Our decision to send Tara back to Duke University was partly influenced by the fact that it had a top-class medical school and some of the best sports surgeons in the world.

If you are injured periodically, you cannot train hard and if you cannot train hard you cannot compete at the highest level. So, after intense family consultations, we decided that it was time for both the children to have surgeries to fix their injuries. Tara went back to Duke University and underwent a lateral release surgery in early 2008 while Venkat underwent surgery in Philadelphia at around the same time to repair a tear in his abdominal wall. After her recovery Tara went back to college tennis, leading Duke to a National Collegiate Athletic Association title at Stanford in May 2009. Venkat, too, was fully fit again after the surgery; he went on to captain Cornell in tennis and lead them to the Ivy League title.

Fortunately, Indira, earning her claim to being the only 'sane' family member among all the tennis 'madness', had all along insisted on the children having a full-fledged education. Despite their crazy schedule, she took it upon herself to play the role of teacher all through their tennis careers. The fact that she was a great teacher and a whiz at mathematics, economics and science ensured that Tara and Venkat were well tutored. Perpetually on the road, both of them were home-schooled by her in their last few years of high school. It worked out very well in the end, with Tara obtaining a PhD in economics from the University of

Oxford and Venkat getting a master's in environmental studies from Columbia University.

Reflections on the women's tennis tour

Having travelled with Tara on the women's tour for almost two years, it is clear to me that 'professional sports', despite the glamour associated with it, is a dog-eat-dog world. The competition is tough and every player competes fiercely to earn WTA points to rise in the global rankings. Only the top 100 women players in the world actually earn a good living out of tennis, while the lower-ranked players struggle to make ends meet, having to pay for their own travel, accommodation as well as that of their coaches and travelling companions. Injuries, all too common for a professional athlete, can seriously hinder or even end a player's career. Ten years after Tara gave up the idea of a professional tennis career due to her chronic knee injury, my understanding is that not much has changed on the women's tennis tour, with the major championships and top players cornering all the resources, and the lesser tournaments and the lower-ranked players still facing uncertain futures. I believe that it is time for the WTA and the ITF to make a serious effort to address this problem. Increasing the prize money for the smaller tournaments would make a difference. Fortunately, both Tara and Venkat had plan Bs and could return to academics.

Back to where I once belonged

Truth be told, it wasn't just the kids who had a safety net to fall back on. I myself still had the civil services career I had paused when joining the World Bank. In May 2008, having finished my stint as a road manager, I returned to Lucknow, to the good old UP cadre.

Ignoring my specialization in water and sanitation, the UP Government posted me as Secretary, Department of Higher Education. Not having much idea about this sector, I focused on curbing the corruption involved in college affiliations, especially for those seeking to set up fly-by-night colleges to teach Bachelor of Education degree courses. I soon got into a conflict with some vested interests while attempting to make the affiliation process merit-based and transparent and, sure enough, within six months, I was transferred to the Forests Department, another sector I had no clue about.

As Principal Secretary, Forests Department, believe it or not, my first three months were focused on attempting to trap and catch two man-eating tigers in different parts of UP. Those were the instructions given to me by the then Cabinet Secretary of UP. He summoned me the day I took up my new job and said that CM Mayawati had ordered that my top priority was to get rid of these tigers since they had already killed many innocent people. While I had no clue how to get rid of tigers, I was pretty sure the CM would get rid of me if I failed in my task, so I decided to find a 'getting rid of tiger expert'! To cut a long story short, my team, the 'expert' and I succeeded in darting and capturing one of the tigers in Lakhimpur Kheri district. This brought me some temporary respite.

Luckily, before the issue of the remaining maneater could come up, however, I was overtaken by another, more pressing, problem. A senior Minister in the state government and I had a dispute about abolishing the transit fee paid to the government by trucks ferrying minerals from mining leases inside the reserved forest area. The matter went to the Cabinet, and CM Mayawati sided with me, much like she had during that memorable Swajal Cabinet meeting 13 years ago, and the transit fee stayed.

Needless to say, this decision did not exactly endear me to the powerful Minister.

In early 2009, I started thinking about returning to the US, where my family was now based. Indira, still on leave from the IRS, was continuing with her PhD in economics from George Washington University, Tara was back at Duke University and Venkat was getting ready to join Cornell University. It did not make much sense for me to continue working in Lucknow while the rest of the family was in the US. Besides, I was keen to get back to the water and sanitation sector which I had left almost three years back. I therefore applied for a new job in the World Bank, went through a couple of interviews through videoconferencing, and was selected. This time, I decided to make a clean break with the IAS and sought voluntary retirement from the government. I took up my new job at the World Bank in Washington DC on 1 June 2009.

8

Run harder if you are at the end of the line

MAKING UP FOR LOST TIME AT THE WORLD BANK

ON MY LAST day in office at the World Bank in 2006, I had met Jamal Saghir, my then boss, for a farewell cup of coffee, where we chatted about my plans as road manager to Tara. As I left his room, he wished me all the best and said, 'Param, you have earned a name for yourself in the Bank, and we could potentially rehire you in the future. But let me warn you that if you do come back, you will have to go back to the end of the line.' Since I was not thinking of returning to the World Bank, I did not pay much heed to his prophetic (as it turned out) words.

Three years later, I did, as warned, go back to the 'end of the line' on returning to the World Bank. I had started out as a Senior Water and Sanitation Specialist when I had joined in 1998 and, now, 11 years later, I was back at the same level. It stung a bit when Mike Webster, the young professional I had recruited 10 years ago in Delhi, now the same grade as me, said to me over lunch during my first week on the job, 'Param, did you have to come back to the Bank at this level? Wasn't it better to remain a senior IAS officer in India, where you could really shake things up?' I laughed it off, saying, 'Mike, the IAS was great, but when you've got to go, you've got to go.'

I felt I didn't need to explain to Mike or anyone else why I had returned to the World Bank. Basically, it did not make sense that I was living alone in Lucknow while my family was in Washington DC. Besides, I was broke, having spent most of my earlier World Bank savings on tennis travel and in supporting the parallel family establishment in Washington DC. Having made a permanent break with the IAS, I was determined to make the most of the situation I now found myself in, and take up my new World Bank job with gusto.

Welcome to Egypt

My new assignment in the World Bank was to work in the water and sanitation sector in the Middle East and North Africa (MENA) region. This job had a different focus from that of my previous assignment with the World Bank three years ago. While my earlier work was focused on distilling and spreading knowledge about water and sanitation amongst our client countries, I was now involved in the core World Bank task of lending money to client countries – what, in Bank parlance, was known as 'operational' work.

Within two weeks of taking up my new job on the sixth floor of the H Building on 19th and H streets, I was asked to join a mission to Cairo, Egypt. In Egypt, the weekend holiday was taken on Fridays and Saturdays. Starting the work week on a Sunday took a little getting used to, but fortunately I felt immediately at home in the offices of the Egyptian institutions that dealt with water and sanitation: the National Office for Potable Water and Sanitary Drainage and the Holding Company for Water and Wastewater. The senior officials warmed up to me when they found out I had been a civil servant in India, virtually 'one of them'. Staying at the Conrad Hotel on the banks of the Nile river and enjoying the delicious Egyptian bread, falafel and kebabs at our team dinner meetings made my first mission to Egypt most memorable.

Climbing up the ladder – now a Task Team Leader

I quickly learned the ropes on that first mission to Cairo, where we were supervising the World Bank-financed Integrated Sewerage and Sanitation Infrastructure Project (referred to as ISSIP1 since there was a second one planned for later), and was appointed the Task Team Leader (TTL) of the project. Although being designated a TTL was itself considered a sign of progress, and supervising the implementation of an ongoing project loan was important, the ultimate achievement for a newly appointed TTL was to 'take a new project loan to the Board'. This referred to the successful completion of a lending operation, the major milestone of which was obtaining the World Bank's Executive Board approval of the project loan.

Commencing regular missions to Egypt, travelling to the Governorates and engaging with the local officials and communities, it soon became apparent that only a limited number of villages across the country were able to safely dispose of wastewater, most of which was being discharged, untreated, into agricultural drains and canals, causing significant pollution. This gap needed to be addressed and I began a dialogue with my government counterparts to scale up the scope of wastewater treatment in the most lagging regions of the country. Our active engagement with key policymakers paid off and, after a few months, the Egyptian government formally requested the World Bank for a new project loan to expand the scope of wastewater treatment in four new Governorates: Menoufia, Sharkeya, Assiut and Sohag. Here was the opportunity to take a new project loan to the Board and I made the most of it. My task team and I travelled extensively in the field in the four Governorates, meeting with government officials and understanding the local context in order to design the project – ISSIP2. Working closely with our Egyptian counterparts, we rapidly designed the new project aimed at providing about 1.2 million people with increased access to improved wastewater systems.

I was handicapped, however, by my inability to speak Arabic with my clients, the Egyptians. Luckily, Mounir Ahmed, the Project Director, spoke English and his favourite phrase was 'Am be struggling', which he used tactically when I pushed him too hard to meet important project preparation deadlines. He was, however, an excellent host and invited me to his house once for a delicious Roza Iftaar meal after a day of Ramadan fasting. His 'fasting', however, was not too rigorous since he periodically delved into his plentiful stock of snacks at the office and fed us on a continual basis. Somewhat overweight then, Mounir looked very fit when I met him in Cairo on my next mission and, when I asked him the secret of his new, trim look, he grinned and proudly said, 'I went in for bariatric surgery last month – am be struggling with my weight no more.'

It never rains but it pours

Working in Egypt with Mounir and the team in preparing the new ISSIP2 project loan with all its complexities was a new experience, made even more challenging by the flaring up of the Arab Spring in Cairo in early 2011. My team and I happened to be in Cairo in January 2011 and we continued with our work despite the growing political unrest. I flew out of the city on 24 January, just in time to escape the mass protests that followed the next day, with the students' occupation of Tahrir Square, a stone's throw from the Conrad Hotel. All incoming and outgoing flights were suspended after that and our missions to Cairo were halted. Despite the subsequent political and administrative challenges in Egypt, we continued to engage with our government counterparts, completed the project loan preparation process in record time, and obtained the approval of the World Bank's Executive Board on 30 June 2011.

The hard work in Egypt paid off and I was asked by my manager in early 2010 to take up another new loan project in Lebanon. So, even though the ISSIP2 project was still under preparation, I jumped at the opportunity to develop, in parallel with the Egyptian project, a new project loan in another country in the region.

While preparing the Egyptian project was a long-drawn-out and laborious process, it paled in comparison to the complexity of the Lebanese project context, both in terms of the country's overall political economy and the technical complexity of the project. My task as TTL was to rapidly develop a $200 million loan to finance a major urban water supply project in Beirut – the Greater Beirut Water Supply Project (GBWSP). For a variety of reasons, the preparation of the project had long been stalled and the Lebanese government was getting impatient. Shuttling between Washington DC, Cairo and now Beirut, I spent more hours flying during that period of 2009–12 than in my entire World Bank career.

My father with me in his lap, my mother next to him, my grandmother behind, and my sisters and cousins standing in the background, Marina beach, Chennai, 1962.

With my sisters, Mina (left) and Indu (right), after I returned from Davidson College in the US, late 1979.

With my new bride, Indira, September 1987.

Boating with Indira and our children, Venkat and Tara, on Nainital lake, 1995.

With fellow officer trainees and local children during the LBSNAA trek to Harkidun, September 1981. I am at the back, with a colleague holding a mug of tea in front of me.

In my chamber as Sub-Divisional Magistrate Dehradun, along with the team, Dehradun, 1985.

In the camp office as District Magistrate, Bijnor, July 1992.

With Tara and Kamran Rizvi, IAS Officer Trainee, to my right, at a Total Literacy Campaign event, Najibabad, Bijnor, 1993.

As Project Director, Swajal, with Xavier Lagrain, Task Team Leader, World Bank, to my right, and Rajinder Singh Bisht, NGO leader, to my left, discussing the project design with the village community at Gangolihat, Pithoragarh, Uttar Pradesh (now in Uttarakhand), 1994.

The Running Air Marshal – Dad, aka Air Marshal P.V. Iyer (Retd) – leading, at age fifty-six, the Agra–Delhi run, October 1985.

Still at it at the age of ninety in the local gym, Bengaluru, 2019.

With the budding tennis pros at Bethesda Chevy-Chase High School, Bethesda, Maryland, 2002.

Tara at an inter-collegiate match at Duke University, Durham, North Carolina, 2006.

Venkat at the Mitsubishi Lancers ITF tournament, Kuala Lumpur, 2007.

Keeping up as road manager – furiously focused at an ITF tournament in Istanbul, 2008.

Dr Indira Iyer – PhD in Economics, George Washington University, 2012.

Living the 'on-the-road' life at the World Bank – standing atop a destroyed Soviet tank in Panjshir Valley, Afghanistan, 2002.

Signing of the loan agreement for the first water and sanitation 'PforR' between the Government of Vietnam and the World Bank, Hanoi, 2013. Seated left: World Bank Country Director Victoria Kwakwa. Seated right: Nguyễn Văn Bình, Chairman of the State Bank of Vietnam. I am standing at the back, third from the left.

Indira and I at the Army Day line-up to meet the Prime Minister (PM). To my left is Raj Chengappa of the India Today Group, to whom the PM said, '*Aapne inko toilet mein dooba diya*,' referring to the December 2019 *India Today* cover photo.

Dad meeting the PM at the Air Force Day reception, October 2018.

A special meeting with the PM for Tara, where he discussed economic development with her, September 2019.

With the PM and the United Nations Secretary-General, Antonio Guterres, at the Mahatma Gandhi International Sanitation Convention, 2 October 2018.

Cartoon by veteran cartoonist Sudhir Dar for the month of August in the Swachh Bharat calendar for 2020.

In the field – digging out *sona khaad* from a twin-pit toilet at Gangadevapalli village, Warangal district, Telangana, February 2017.

At a school rally in Dhamtari district, Chhattisgarh, 2018.

Team Swachh Bharat when India was declared Open Defecation Free (ODF), on the 150th birth anniversary of Mahatma Gandhi, 2 October 2019, Ahmedabad.

With Swachh Bharat Ambassador Amitabh Bachchan at the launch of the Darwaza Band campaign, Mumbai, 2017.

With Swachh Bharat Ambassador Akshay Kumar at the launch of the twin-pit toilet technology campaign, also starring Bhumi Pednekar, New Delhi, 2017.

On 'Off the Cuff' with Shekhar Gupta of *The Print*, Mumbai, 2018.

5 a.m. golf sessions at the Delhi Golf Club with (left to right) K.P. Krishnan, former Secretary to the Government of India; Amitabh Kant, CEO, NITI Aayog; and Rajiv Mehrishi, former Comptroller and Auditor General of India, New Delhi, 2019.

The PM launching the Rashtriya Swachhata Kendra (RSK) at Delhi on 8 August 2020. The RSK is an interactive experience-sharing centre about the Swachh Bharat Mission.

Chairing a meeting of the Empowered Group on supply chain and logistics management of essential items during the COVID-19 pandemic, August 2020.

The main objective of the project was to increase the provision of potable water to the residents of the city. The project involved the implementation of a technically challenging infrastructural marvel: the boring of a water tunnel that was 24 km long and 3 m in diameter through a rocky mountain. The non-engineering aspects of project preparation were equally challenging in Lebanon, and I had to quickly get up to speed with the task of engaging with the different wings and factions within the Lebanese government. Fortunately, I had a great team, which included the young and dynamic Claire Kfouri, an MIT-trained wastewater engineer. Claire, a Canadian-Lebanese national, was not only technically sound, but also knew the Lebanese political context intimately. The fact that she was fluent in both French and Arabic made engagement with our Lebanese government counterparts even more effective.

While staying and working in the cosmopolitan city of Beirut was a pleasure, the most enjoyable part of my stint in Lebanon was driving through the beautiful Bekaa valley in the eastern part of the country, where the water source and tunnel site of our project were located. The icing on the cake was the delicious Lebanese food. It was my first experience tasting hummus and tabbouleh, and also sampling all kinds of shawarmas. The choicest of Mediterranean fruits – grapes, apricots, plums and peaches – were also always available at roadside cafes. The real 'fruit' of my achievement as a TTL in Lebanon, however, was the satisfaction of taking another loan project to the Board in record time – only 10 months. The GBWSP was approved by the Executive Board on 16 December 2010 – six months earlier, in fact, than the ISSIP2 loan.

My great leap forward – relocating to Hanoi

After working for about three years on Egypt and Lebanon, with two new projects loans to the Board under my belt, and now being taken much more seriously by the 'operations' folks in the World Bank, I felt fully qualified to seek a promotion and thought it time to make that big leap forward. I applied for the position of a Lead Water and Sanitation Specialist, a higher-level position based in Hanoi, Vietnam. Thanks to my strengthened 'operational' credentials, I got selected for the job. The Vietnam position gave me a broader mandate than just water and sanitation: I was appointed the Cluster Head of the World Bank's huge 'water, sanitation and urban lending' portfolio in Vietnam, a major focus country in the East Asia region.

After proudly attending Indira's PhD convocation at the George Washington University in the summer of 2012, I was ready to start working on the World Bank's Vietnam programme. We relocated to Hanoi in September 2012 and again became a globally dispersed family, now distributed over three continents: Tara pursuing graduate studies in economics in Oxford, England; Venkat doing undergraduate studies at Cornell University, USA; and Indira and I based in Hanoi. The two of us lived in a fully serviced apartment, only a 15-minute commute from the World Bank's downtown office.

From quantity to quality of operations

Being located in the World Bank's country office in Hanoi and having the comparative advantage of 'being on call' and engaging with our government clients on an ongoing basis made a big difference to the quality of our work. I found the senior Vietnamese government officials extremely practical and efficient. They were pleasant to work with, always willing to try out new ideas and approaches, and were fully accessible. In Hanoi, I could even meet the vice-ministers (equivalent to Secretaries to the Government of India) in key ministries at short notice. This easy accessibility of the senior-most Vietnamese civil servants taught me a lesson that would stand me in good stead a few years later when I rejoined the Indian government.

> **Pro-Tip:** Be accessible to your team and your clients. It breaks down many communication barriers.

I had a wonderful team in Hanoi, mainly consisting of Vietnamese staff, who quickly brought me up to speed with the local way of doing business and also introduced me to our major clients at national and provincial levels. Giang Nguyen, in particular, my team assistant, was my guide when it came to learning the dos and don'ts of local Vietnamese customs, including never disturbing team members with office work during the most important festival of the year – Tet! I also learned to enjoy some Vietnamese delicacies like Pho, a kind of noodle soup. A little surprised that I was a teetotaller but happy that I was not a vegetarian, Giang said it was fine for me to not join our clients for vodka toasts over dinner as long as I did not hurt their sensibilities further by also refusing the food on offer. On one occasion in the Northern Mountains, this almost turned out to be a devil's bargain: I had the tough choice between sampling either fried bees or the local rice liquor. Despite never having tasted alcohol, I was almost tempted to go for the rice liquor but, at the last minute, went for the fried bees. I did not try that again!

The birth of the PforR

My first lending operation in Vietnam was a unique one. In a collaborative engagement with our government counterparts in the Ministry of Agriculture and Rural Development (MARD), my team and I designed the first loan in the World Bank's entire global water and sanitation portfolio to use the brand new PforR (Programme for Results) lending instrument. This $200 million loan to Vietnam to provide clean water and improved sanitation in eight provinces in the Red River Delta was approved by the World Bank's Executive Board on 1 November 2012. This was now the third time I had taken a project loan to the Board and the first using the new PforR lending instrument.

The PforR lending instrument introduced a radically new approach to the World Bank's lending, directly linking disbursement of the loan to the delivery of verifiable results. Previous loans had focused more on loan disbursement than actual achievement of the planned outcomes of the project. This results-based approach to financing development programmes has proved to be very useful in terms of incentivizing and optimizing outcomes, and is increasingly being adopted by government-funded programmes across the world. In India, too, results-based financing is becoming the norm, especially for infrastructure projects.

Since we were traversing uncharted territory in developing this project loan using the brand new PforR lending instrument, it became imperative to have a first-rate team who could bring different skills and experiences to the table. I therefore set about searching the world for the right professionals and succeeded in creating a 'global dream team'. The core members of this multinational team were co-TTL, Hanoi-based Hoa Hoang; the young and dynamic Victor Vasquez, a Spaniard and one of the Bank's elite Young Professionals; American Lee Travers, one of the best water economists in the World Bank; and Professor Barbara Evans from the University of Leeds in the UK, one of the top water and sanitation experts in the world. Working closely with the project provinces and MARD, we designed and prepared the new project in record time.

Working in Hanoi turned out to be a productive period in terms of developing new project loans. Having gained the confidence of our country clients, I took two more PforR lending operations to the Board, the second being a $250 million loan, which was approved by the Board on 5 June 2014 to fund an urban development project in the Northern Mountains. The third PforR lending operation I led as TTL in Vietnam was the rural sanitation and water supply project in the Northern Mountains and Central Highlands, which was approved by the Board on 15 November 2015.

The fringe benefit of travelling to some of the more remote provinces for project preparation was that I got to visit many fascinating places, including the site of the famous battle of Dien Bien Phu in Dien Bien province, where the invincible Vietnamese General Ziap defeated the French army in a decisive clash in 1954.

15 August 2014 – a day to remember

It was while Indira and I were in Hanoi that a tipping point occurred in my life and career. The date was 15 August 2014 and we were sitting in our Hanoi apartment. It was a working day, and Indira – now working for the International Finance Corporation in Vietnam – and I had taken half a day off to watch, on TV, the new Indian PM's first Independence Day speech from the Red Fort in New Delhi. About 45 minutes into his speech, Indira and I were jolted into amazement: PM Modi, in his first major nationwide address, was talking about the lack of toilets in the country and the indignity of women and girls having to defecate in the open. This was unheard of, especially in India, where such a topic was rarely mentioned in public, let alone during a prime ministerial national address. The PM went on to announce that India would launch a Swachh Bharat (Clean India) Mission, and, as a tribute to the father of the nation, rid the country of open defecation by 2 October 2019, the 150th birth anniversary of Mahatma Gandhi. I was beside myself with excitement and recall saying to my wife, 'How do I get back to India and join this programme?' That was wishful thinking at the time, and I continued working in Hanoi for another nine months before taking up my next assignment in Washington DC.

Getting back to DC (another promotion!)

After completing three years in Hanoi, Indira and I started thinking about returning to Washington DC. By now, I had become one of the World Bank's most experienced TTLs and could think of moving up the career ladder. I thus applied for the position of Water Practice Manager for the South Asia region, which would also include working on India. Since the stakes were higher this time and the position much in demand, I prepared thoroughly for the job interview, and in particular for a suitable response to the standard opening question asked in all such interviews: 'Why are you interested in the job and what makes you think you are the best candidate for it?' Fortunately, I came up with the winning reply: 'This job is tailor-made for me and I strongly believe that I am the *right* person, at the *right* time and at the *right* place for it.' The interview continued for another 20 minutes, during which I backed my seemingly immodest opening statement with substance, and adequately fielded the other questions posed to me. I got the job and took over as the Practice Manager in May 2015. I had now graduated from TTL-ship to management.

> **Pro-Tip:** Make sure you practise well for the answer to the standard opening questions in all interviews: 'Why are you interested in this job?' and 'What makes you think you are the best candidate for it?'

My new job entailed managing a team of about 40 professional staff, most of whom were scattered across six countries in the South Asia region. We had a $6 billion lending portfolio for water and sanitation projects, the biggest across all regions of the World Bank. My first mission to South Asia as Practice Manager in June 2015 was a three-week lightning trip to six countries: India, Afghanistan, Pakistan, Bangladesh, Sri Lanka and Nepal. Joining my TTLs in engaging with their government counterparts in these countries, I again found my IAS background coming in handy, since our clients in these erstwhile British-colonized countries could easily relate to our common civil service heritage. In fact, the Additional Chief Secretary of Sindh province in Pakistan and I hit it off very well, swapping the usual civil service stories of our respective days as DMs. He hosted me to some superb Frontier cuisine in a Karachi restaurant after which I travelled to the Sukkur barrage via Larkana (the hometown of the country's foremost political family, the Bhuttos), where we sampled excellent guavas, reddish pink inside, very much like those grown in Allahabad.

Working as a Practice Manager out of Washington DC with most of my team in different time zones in distant South Asia was challenging. I used to reach the office at 6.30 a.m. to connect to team members in South Asia for whom it was late afternoon. The benefit of getting in so early from our house in Bethesda was the sparse traffic on the Washington Beltway. After parking my car in a K Street garage, I would walk across to the Starbucks on Pennsylvania Street near the White House, pick up a tall coffee and an 'everything' bagel before walking to my little corner room on the tenth floor of the Main Complex building of the World Bank on 18th and H streets. It was here, one early February 2016 morning, that I received an email from Delhi informing me of some incredibly exciting news, and my life and career took another completely new turn.

INSIDER (2016–2020)

28 February 2016

EWR ✈ DEL

CO 82

I WAS AT Newark airport, once again checking in for a direct flight to Delhi, this time with Continental Airlines. Knowing there would not be much to eat on the 13-hour flight to Delhi, I grabbed a Subway sandwich and Coke before boarding the flight. Cramped in a middle seat, I tried to while away the time by watching an old movie, *Where Eagles Dare*, based on the book by Alistair McLean, one of my favourite thriller writers.

After the movie, I dozed off for a while and then tried to shake off the stiffness by walking up and down the aisle. I thought about the job at the World Bank I had left behind and about the new job I was taking up as Secretary to the Government of India, at the Ministry of Drinking Water and Sanitation. It was going to be a big change in many ways. From leading a small team of 40 people, I was going to be the Secretary of a Union ministry with hundreds of staff members. From being responsible for delivering loans to South Asian countries for water and sanitation projects,

I was returning to my own country to join a national flagship programme which would transform people's lives, especially those of women and girls.

Landing in Delhi early the next morning, I took an airport taxi to the Uttar Pradesh Sadan in Chanakyapuri, where I had stayed many times while visiting Delhi from Lucknow on official business. Jet-lagged and wide awake, I had a nostalgic cup of sweet masala chai and decided to go for a run along my old Shantipath route. Returning to a nice breakfast of aloo parathas and curd, I felt completely at home and all set to start the day.

9

Carpe Diem – Be an opportunist

MY 'LATERAL ENTRY' INTO THE WORLD'S LARGEST BEHAVIOUR
CHANGE PROGRAMME

THERE ARE MOMENTS in everyone's life when opportunity comes knocking. It comes with challenges, risks and inconveniences. But not everyone is able to recognize an opportunity and act swiftly to seize it before it passes by – carpe diem, as the Roman poet Horace said, or 'seize the day'.

Getting 'the call' and grabbing the opportunity with both hands

My opportunity came in early December 2015, when, as the World Bank's Practice Manager for South Asia, I was on a mission to Sri Lanka to support my TTL in supervising an ongoing World Bank-funded dam project in the picturesque town of Kandy. I received an unexpected call from a New Delhi number asking me to meet the Cabinet Secretary, the most senior civil servant in the country, on my next visit to Delhi. I was intrigued, and transitted through Delhi on my return to Washington. When I reached Delhi a few days later, I met the Cabinet Secretary, P.K. Sinha. After the initial pleasantries, Mr Sinha cut to the chase and asked me if I had considered returning to the government. He informed me that the incumbent Secretary of the Ministry of Drinking Water and Sanitation (MDWS) had recently resigned, and the government was looking for a replacement. 'We're looking this time to recruit a domain expert, not necessarily the usual generalist from the IAS,' he said. 'You have the right sector experience plus, in a sense, you are an insider–outsider, having worked for long in government, with full knowledge of how our system works.'

It took a couple of moments for his words to register. This was more than a dream come true. Being Secretary of the MDWS would mean I would be in-charge of implementing the Swachh Bharat Mission (SBM), the largest sanitation programme ever attempted anywhere in the world. I remembered the urge to be part of this amazing initiative the day I first heard PM Modi announce it from the Red Fort in 2014. I was excited and intrigued since, to the best of my knowledge, no previous government had ever laterally recruited an ex-civil servant at the level of Secretary to the Government of India. I immediately conveyed my interest in the job and was advised that a decision would be taken after due process was followed.

On the long flight back to DC the following day, I kept thinking about the incredible opportunity which was potentially coming my way. I was cautiously confident that I had the credentials to take up the position of a Secretary to the Government of India. While I had been out of the IAS for many years, I had spent that time gaining invaluable experience and knowledge from the world over, which could be applied to the recently launched SBM. With my civil service background and understanding of the context, I was sure of hitting the ground running if selected for the job. Animated discussions ensued at home with Indira after I reached Washington, but at office I continued with my World Bank work as though nothing had happened. In fact, nothing did happen for many weeks and there was no news from Delhi of any further developments.

Having not heard anything by the end of January, I had more or less given up hope. Then, early morning on 3 February 2016, just after reaching my office at my usual time of 6.30 a.m., armed with my coffee and an 'everything' bagel, I received an email from Delhi from an IAS batchmate, which simply said: 'Congratulations, and welcome back to India – your appointment order has been put up on the Department of Personnel website.' I immediately went to the website and saw the following order posted on it: 'The Appointments Committee of the Cabinet has approved the appointment of Shri Parameswaran Iyer, IAS (voluntarily retired) (UP: 1981) as Secretary, Ministry of Drinking Water and Sanitation, on contract basis for a period of two years from the date of assumption of charge of the post or till further orders, whichever is earlier.' My excitement knew no bounds, and most of my World Bank colleagues were very happy for me as well. Over the next few weeks, Indira and I began the winding up of our Washington establishment, including putting our house out to rent. Indira stayed back for some time to complete the process and I left for Delhi in the last week of February.

Carving out the goal

I reached Delhi on 28 February 2016, two days before I was to formally take charge at the MDWS on 1 March. I immediately sought time with my predecessor, Vijayalaxmi Joshi, to understand the contours of the SBM and the MDWS context before I formally took charge. She readily agreed to meet me for a cup of coffee the next day.

> **Pro-Tip**: Try not to walk into a new assignment cold. Do your due diligence before you begin.

I met Ms Joshi at the Delhi Gymkhana Club. I was bursting with curiosity and excitement about my new job and she was kind enough to give me a status update about the SBM, describing the planning and preparation that had gone into the launch of the programme and the current implementation status. The SBM had by then been going on for about 17 months and Ms Joshi felt that there was a need to define the goal of the programme more explicitly. There was also a need to clearly differentiate between the rural and urban components of the SBM, the former being much larger in scale and under the MDWS and the latter smaller and under the Ministry of Urban Development.

Swachhata (general cleanliness) can mean a lot of things to a lot of people. For an urban dweller the concept of *swachhata* is usually associated with the efficient and appropriate disposal of waste generated from our households by the municipal body. The lack of *swachhata* is probably manifested by an ugly-looking neighbourhood garbage dump.

In rural India, the *swachhata* imperative was very different – eliminating the rampant practice of open defecation. Apart from the disgusting sight and smell of human excreta lying all around rural areas in India, having to go out in the open to defecate was an insult to people's dignity, especially of women, as well as a security hazard since they could only go out to relieve themselves in the dark. While successive governments over the 67 years since India's independence had paid only lip service to tackling the problem of open defecation, PM Modi had not only appreciated the true extent of the problem, but confronted the issue head-on and declared that India would be rid of the practice of open defecation in five years.

With only three and a half years to the deadline announced by the PM, it was important to focus, laser-like, on the target. Instead of spreading our resources thin, therefore, we simply had to go all out to ensure that every Indian had access to a toilet and also used it, thereby making the country open defecation free (ODF) by 2 October 2019. To do this for 550 million rural Indians, we would need to unleash a massive behaviour change campaign cum toilet construction programme.

Making every day count, literally

I still remember my first day on the job, 1 March 2016, when I was driven to Paryavaran Bhawan in Delhi's CGO complex. In keeping with its name, 'paryavaran' (environment), our building was green in colour, and visible from a distance. When I arrived, a couple of office boys were waiting to open the door of my car, carry my bag and keep the elevator open and waiting for me. On the fourth floor, I was received at the elevator by my Principal Private Secretary (PPS), Surendra Gosain, and taken to my office.

With decades of experience in the government, my PPS was in for a rude shock with my 'non-sarkari' style of working. He and the other office staff were scandalized that I reached office at 8.30 a.m. daily (as opposed to the leisurely 9.30–10 a.m. arrival time of some other senior officers) and typically left at around 8 p.m., after extracting every ounce of work from the workday. Used to my Washington DC work routine, I was actually toying with the idea of reaching office even earlier than 8.30 a.m., but Indira talked me out of it. 'I think 8.30 a.m. is early enough,' she said. 'Reaching office earlier than that will ensure that your staff hate you.' So, I stuck to 8.30 a.m. An early start to the day had two clear advantages for me: first, I had some 'alone' quality time to think and plan the day's agenda and, second, if I reached office at 8.30 a.m., it sent a signal to the other officers to get there by at least 9 or 9.15 a.m.

Pro-Tip: Punctuality is one of the most appreciated attributes. Your boss always keeps note of when you reach your office, especially if you are new to the job.

Back to day one: on entering my office premises, I saw that my name, in bold letters, was engraved on a board on the wall outside the office. The name was followed by the three 'magic' letters – 'IAS' – after it. The office itself was extremely large, with wooden flooring, a few sofas and a huge table and chair. A large Indian flag stood next to the table. And on the other side of the table was a big brown board which had the names and tenures of all of my illustrious predecessors. Having got used to a cubicle of a room without a full-time personal assistant in the World Bank in Washington DC, I found the largesse the Government of India provided to its Secretaries, by way of office space and staff, overwhelming. While I soaked it all in, I remember telling Gosain to remove the letters IAS from the board outside the office. His jaw dropped in surprise. 'But, sir, why should I remove them? Aren't you an IAS officer?' My reply was: 'I used to be, but am no longer. Believe it or not, I am a non-IAS Secretary to the Government of India.'

One of the first things I did after entering my new office was to ask for a white board to be put up on the wall behind me. On the white board I jotted down a few numbers: 1, 729, 44%, 40,000. Gosain was confused. I told him we had a big task ahead of us and I intended to make every day count; this white board would serve as a reminder for it. This was, once again, one of Indira's great suggestions.

The numbers on the white board were the number of days I had been on the job, the number of days I had left in my initial two-year contract, the existing sanitation coverage in rural India, and the number of villages declared ODF so far. The targets for the third and fourth numbers were 100 per cent and

6,00,000 respectively. I asked Gosain to update these numbers first thing every morning. Over the years I spent on the job, I asked every new visitor to my office to guess what the numbers on that white board signified. While a few guessed the rapidly increasing rural sanitation coverage and the number of ODF villages, they were always stumped by the first two numbers, which indicated the number of days I had spent on the job and the days left.

On my second day on the job, I sought time with Nripendra Mishra, Principal Secretary to the PM, to discuss the ODF goal I had chalked out. R.S. Sharma, Chairman of the Telecom Regulatory Authority of India, was also in the room and Mr Mishra introduced me to him, saying, 'Parameswaran has just returned from the World Bank to do some real work in India.' I duly noted the quip. With an incredibly sharp mind and the ability to always come directly to the point, Mr Mishra conducted ruthlessly efficient meetings and was always on top of his game. Over time, as the SBM made progress, he became a strong ally and mentor. His opening question at our later meetings became a standing joke between us: 'Parameswaran, how is your defecation going?' He was referring, of course, to the progress of the SBM and its goal of making India ODF. My standard deadpan reply was: 'It's going fine, sir.'

'Please introduce me to the big boss'

It had been a few weeks since I had joined as Secretary, MDWS, and many of my family and friends had begun asking me if I had met the PM yet. I had to admit this had not happened so far. One day, I went to meet Amitabh Kant, an old college friend and the dynamic CEO of the NITI Aayog, the Government of India's premier policy think tank, and he suggested I seek an appointment with the PM. 'Call Rajeev Topno, his Private Secretary, and ask to meet the PM,' Amitabh advised. I did so and Rajeev told me he would get back to me soon. I waited for a fortnight but did not hear back from him. On 21 April, on the occasion of Civil Services Day, there was an evening reception at the grand Rashtrapati Bhawan Convention Centre, which was attended by the President of India, the Vice-President and the PM. It was a large gathering and many of the invitees were crowding around the PM, hoping for a word with him. Keeping my distance from the throng, I chatted with Hasmukh Adhia, the Revenue Secretary and my Gujarat cadre IAS batchmate, who had worked very closely with the PM in the latter's previous role of Chief Minister of Gujarat. 'Come on, Hasmukh,' I finally said, 'can you introduce me to the PM?' He was rather surprised to learn I hadn't met the PM yet, and immediately walked me over to where PM Modi was standing, talking to the Cabinet Secretary. 'Sir,' Hasmukh interjected, 'I would like to introduce you to Parameswaran Iyer, my batchmate and the new Secretary for Drinking Water and Sanitation.'

I greeted the PM with a namaste and said something about what an honour it was for me to meet him. With a straight face he responded, '*Aap wohi hai na jo IAS se bhaag kar bahar chale gaye the?*' (Aren't you the one who had run away abroad from the IAS?) I was a little disconcerted but, luckily, he then smiled and said, 'I know you have asked for an appointment with me – I will meet you soon.' I marvelled at the PM's sharp memory: his remembering I had quit the IAS and that I had asked for an appointment with him. 'He has an incredible memory and remembers every single detail,' confirmed Hasmukh as we walked away. I was thrilled with that brief encounter and could finally tell my family and friends I had met PM Modi, and that he knew my name.

A few days later, I got a call from Rajeev Topno and was told that the PM would meet me on 30 April at his South Block office. I remember preparing hard over the weekend for the meeting. I was excited and rehearsed what I planned to say to him multiple times. When the day arrived, I felt reasonably confident, until I was ushered into his huge office in South Block. He was seated at a big desk at the other end of the room, and as I walked up to him, I realized I was a little nervous.

I greeted the PM with a namaste and he smiled and asked me to take a seat. I started out by explaining why I had left the IAS and joined the World Bank in Washington DC. 'It was a family decision, Sir. The main reason was that my wife and I wanted to give our two tennis-playing children the best opportunity to get world-class coaching and training facilities to become professional tennis players.' He listened patiently as I spoke.

After a while, the PM asked me what my initial thoughts were about the SBM and its implementation so far. I gave him my assessment and shared my ideas about launching a massive behaviour change campaign to encourage toilet usage. He nodded and made a humorous reference to his experience with rural sanitation as a volunteer in Morvi, Gujarat, almost 50 years ago, when he found that many of the villagers provided with toilets were using them as goat shelters. 'Behaviour change is indeed the key,' said the PM. After a few more minutes of pleasantries, I left the room inspired, with the PM's parting words ringing in my ears: '*Jaiye, aur Bharat ko swachh banaiye.*' (Go ahead and make India clean.)

10

Belief is a necessary condition for success

RALLYING THE TROOPS TOWARDS THE 'IMPOSSIBLE' GOAL

LEADERS OFTEN ARTICULATE lofty goals. Whether they lead countries, companies or other organizations, they usually declare their vision and expect their teams to translate them into reality. One of the most common pitfalls in such a situation, however, is the lack of congruence between the articulated vision of the leader and the level of belief, enthusiasm and understanding of the teams tasked with implementing the vision. The lack of belief in achieving the goal can become a self-fulfilling prophecy. As they say, if you think you can, you will; if you think you can't, you won't!

The 'Big Hairy Audacious Goal'

When teams are faced with a seemingly insurmountable target, such as PM Modi's vision of an ODF India by 2 October 2019, they tend to subconsciously dismiss the targets as unachievable. With negligible progress on sanitation over the past 70 years and with 550 million people defecating in the open in rural India, I could understand the hesitation in the team I inherited. Only if the team truly believed the target was achievable *and* was fully dedicated to the cause, would they, one way or another, find a way to succeed. And so, when leaders put out a 'Big Hairy Audacious Goal', or BHAG – a term popularized by management guru Jim Collins – a team of believers has a much greater chance of achieving it compared to a team of sceptics. As the newly appointed Secretary of the MDWS, and thereby accountable for the delivery of the PM's BHAG of an ODF India, I had to quickly make a binary choice: whether to be a believer or a non-believer. There was not an iota of doubt in my mind in this regard: I was a hardcore believer and now I had to make sure the rest of my team believed too.

Seeing is believing

The first thing I decided to do was travel to the field and understand for myself what the real challenge was. Within a week of joining as Secretary, MDWS, I went on some quick visits to a few states, starting with Gujarat. In Ahmedabad, I met the CM, Anandibai Patel, who seemed knowledgeable about the sanitation sector and went into the intricacies of the twin-leach-pit toilet model. She suggested I visit the Ishwarbhai Patel Environmental Sanitation Institute (ESI) in the city, where I could see for myself the different toilet technologies and their applications in rural areas. At the ESI, I was immediately struck by the utility of the twin-pit toilet model, its low cost and how it seemed the most appropriate for rural India. I still had a few reservations about whether rural communities were really convinced about the safe disposal of waste from this type of toilet and the associated stigma of having to clean one's own toilet, but more of that later. During my Gujarat visit I also went to Sabarkanta district and interacted with a few rural householders who did not have toilets. When I asked the women of the house if they desired to have toilets, there was a mixed response: some of them seemed indifferent to my question while others, mostly younger women, showed interest in having a toilet at home. The men, on the other hand, were surprised the question was even being posed to them: as far as they were concerned, it was perfectly all right to defecate in the open. 'We have been doing this for ages,' said an elderly man.

I then went on visits to two states – UP and Bihar, each with a sanitation coverage of less than 30 per cent – which lagged far behind other states in terms of toilet coverage. On an early morning visit to some villages in Unnao district in UP, I found rows and rows of villagers (mainly men) in the fields just off the main highway, nonchalantly defecating in the open, each with a plastic bottle of water beside him. After visiting three or four villages and seeing (and smelling) the same unpleasant phenomenon, I went back to one of the villages later in the day for a meeting at the Panchayat Ghar, the local government office, with the pradhan and the assembled villagers. I was glad to see plenty of women in the audience.

I came straight to the point: 'Pradhanji, why is everybody defecating in the open – shouldn't all of you have toilets at home and use them? Haven't you heard of PM Modi's call for a Swachh Bharat and an open defecation free country?' Averting his eyes, the pradhan replied, somewhat sheepishly, 'Sahib, I have heard of Swachh Bharat, but we are used to defecating in the open – we have been doing it for centuries. Why should we change now?' Another man piped up: 'I don't think that it is a hygienic practice to defecate in a toilet inside or near our homes. The further from our houses we defecate, the cleaner and purer they will be.' There were murmurs of assent to the latter's statement.

As I persisted in asking more questions on the topic, an elderly gentleman put his hand up, introduced himself as a retired soldier, and said he had a toilet at home which his family and he used. I complimented him on this practice and said, 'There are good reasons why defecating in the open is not good. One of them is that human excreta lying in the open pollutes the groundwater and nearby water bodies. Further, flies sit on human excreta and then carry it to the food you eat, which causes disease.' I added, 'The simplest way of separating human contact with human excreta is by containing it in a toilet at home.'

At this, a young lady, head duly covered, hesitatingly spoke up: 'I would like to have a toilet at home, since I feel unsafe going out to the fields in the dark to defecate.' I was just about to endorse her opinion but was beaten to it by a teenage girl, who spoke so softly that I could barely hear her: 'Me too.'

I could see there were already some local 'champions' in the community committed to playing their part in ending the age-old habit of defecating in the open. The challenge now was to trigger the entire community into jointly committing themselves to ending open defecation and, in the process, demanding and using toilets. I saw more or less the same situation on a visit to villages in Nalanda district, Bihar.

As I returned to Delhi, the magnitude of the task ahead of me started to sink in. There were two daunting challenges. The first was the sheer *scale* of the problem: changing the behaviour of 550 million rural Indians used to defecating in the open, coupled with making available over 100 million toilets for them to use. The second was the need to operate with *speed*: the task at hand, which had not been completed in the 70 years since Independence, now had to be achieved in less than five years. The good news was that some people in rural communities, especially women and children, already believed that the pernicious practice of open defecation should stop. Our job would be to help spread that belief across the entire rural community.

But, before we could embark on the ambitious venture of changing behaviour at the grassroots level, I had to first convert my team, and others in the Government of India, into believers.

Spreading the belief

I clearly remember my initial discussions with senior officers of my Ministry during my early days on the job. Other than one or two of the younger, more enthusiastic officers, most of them held that since sanitation, according to the Constitution of India, was not a federal but a state subject, its implementation was the responsibility of the states. Our job at the Government of India level, argued my most senior officer, was to 'support' the states with the right policy architecture, technical assistance and sufficient funding. He felt we should focus from a distance – read Delhi – on the overall monitoring of the programme and let the states get on with the job. I was also reminded that at the time of the start of the SBM, in October 2014, the country had a rural sanitation coverage of less than 40 per cent, and that there was no way we could go from 39 per cent to 100 per cent in just five years. He added, for good measure, that such a wildly ambitious programme had never even been attempted in such a short time anywhere in the world.

I was not buying this argument. First of all, I genuinely believed in the merits of the PM's vision of an ODF India, which would radically transform the quality of lives of, in particular, women and girls in the country who had to suffer the indignity and insecurity of defecating in the open. Second, I was not foolish enough to start off my exciting new job on the wrong foot by trying to explain to the PM why his goal could not be achieved. And, third, after my recent field visits to villages in three states, I was sure that, despite the many challenges, there was potential to scale up behaviour change and use the appropriate toilet technology for providing toilets to our rural population. But, before we could begin working with the states, districts and communities, I needed to shake up the laissez-faire environment in the ministry and, for this, new blood was required.

> **Pro-Tip:** It is not always possible to nudge status quo-ists. Make a choice as to whether it is worth your while to invest in such people, or bite the bullet and go out to find some true believers.

Finding a team of believers

Fortunately, like in the Swajal project, I was once again given carte blanche to get a new set of officers and, after casting the recruitment net far and wide, I handpicked the following crew of 'believers' to join the 'new normal' in the Ministry: (i) Arun Baroka, a knowledgeable and experienced IAS officer from the AGMUT (Arunachal Pradesh–Goa–Mizoram–Union Territory) cadre, (ii) Akshay Rout, a dynamic officer from the Indian Information Service, (iii) V. Radha, a talented and innovative IAS officer from the Maharashtra cadre, (iv) Samir Kumar, a seasoned economist from the Indian Economic Service, (v) Hiranya

Borah, a well-regarded statistician from the Indian Statistical Service, and (vi) Yugal Joshi, an environmental engineer from the Indian Railway Protection Force. We already had Nipun Vinayak, a young and energetic IAS officer who was passionate about sanitation, and were also fortunate to inherit Seemantinee Sengupta, our calm management information system (MIS) head; O.P. Agarwal, who provided the MIS technology backbone for the SBM operation; and Junaid, a long-standing consultant who was the institutional memory for the pre-SBM sanitation programmes.

Each of our core team members had his or her own strengths, but their one common feature was the fire in their belly. The other unifying thread that bound us together was that we genuinely believed the goal of achieving an ODF India by 2019 was not that impossible after all.

This can-do attitude of our team was one of the reasons for the rapid progress towards the SBM goal. We also brought in two teams of consultants, with some talented professionals, to work with the officers on technical matters and to help monitor the programme. These were in-sourced teams of professionals from third-party agencies, led by experts: Anand Shekhar, a seasoned water and sanitation professional who understood the ground reality of sanitation in India like no other, headed one of the consultant teams; and Sharad Kumar, a hard-working management expert, whose team worked with the states to closely monitor the programme in real time.

My front office team

In addition to bringing in a fresh set of government officers and consultant teams, I also decided to strengthen my personal office team with a few young professionals with fresh and uninhibited ideas. While my veteran PPS, Surendra Gosain, was an outstanding source of support and advice, I thought it important to add a core team of idealistic youngsters. I had always worked with young professionals during my time in the World Bank, and had reaped big benefits from this approach. Having a core team of special assistants in the office of a Secretary to the Government of India, however, was a relatively new concept and there was no ready precedent that I could draw upon to bring young talent from outside the government into the front office.

As I was thinking of how this team would materialize, I saw an opportunity when I met R. Venkataraman, Managing Trustee of the Tata Trusts, at a dinner event during my first week on the job. I got chatting with him and threw out a feeler as to whether an organization as celebrated as the Tata Trusts would be interested in contributing to the PM's flagship programme. I followed up this opening gambit by telling him I was sure there were many young and bright professionals with management backgrounds and from top universities working at the Tata Trusts, and that I wanted a couple of such young professionals to be a part of my office team at the MDWS. I emphasized that this would be a unique opportunity for the Tata Trusts to contribute pro bono to a flagship national programme. As it turned out, this was an offer he could not refuse.

About a week later, I had three young professionals in my office: Mahima Vashisht, an engineer with an MBA from the Indian Institute of Management, Bengaluru, and a few years of experience in the Indian Information Service; Vineet Jain, a chemical engineer from Mumbai with an MBA from the Faculty of Management Studies, Delhi, and part of the prestigious Tata Administrative Service; and Rohan Manchanda, the youngest of the three, an engineer from the Birla Institute of Technology and Science. Mahima and Vineet have been with me throughout the journey. Rohan moved on to pursue an MBA a couple of years later and was replaced by Karishma Kadyan, who had a double master's from Jawaharlal Nehru University (in languages) and from Universitat Autonoma de Barcelona, Spain (in anthropology), and came out of the Zila Swachh Bharat Prerak (ZSBP) programme (described in the following chapter). All of them were true believers in the mission and, with their energy, innovative ideas and ability to relentlessly follow through on my instructions, these young professionals significantly enhanced the effectiveness of the Secretary's office.

Disruption in the workplace

Along with creating an MDWS team of believers with energy, it was important to develop a new work ethic, a sense of purpose and a correspondingly conducive environment.

Some disruption in the workplace was called for. The now established early start to the workday, a mini disruption in itself, gave a new sense of purpose to the programme. Staff members started coming in earlier than before and, in many cases, leaving after dusk. The cumbersome paper files were scrapped and, in a radical step for the time, we switched to an efficient electronic e-office system of file movement. With this, my fellow officers and I ended up spending much less time pushing files and much more on the programme and its goals. Although seniority was always respected, I tried my best to flatten the usual hierarchy of a government office and interacted with the entire team on a regular basis. Starting with daily meetings with the entire team for Mission 100 (making 100 districts ODF in my first year), we moved onto Mission 300 meetings in Year 2 and then Mission

Quality and Sustainability meetings from Year 3 onwards. These meetings were attended by all team members. In the large conference room adjacent to my office, 30 to 40 people would come together for a free exchange of information and ideas as well as daily progress monitoring. A war room was also set up to track the advancement towards the ODF goal, with each team member given a set of districts and states to monitor. A new sense of energy and belief became palpable within a few months of my joining and, as results started coming in, the belief in the goal was reinforced and grew stronger.

I also adopted a fairly democratic way of conducting meetings. While the senior officers in the Ministry would sit with me at the head of the table, the discussions were open to all team members, including consultants. Everyone was expected to focus on the discussion at hand, not conduct side conversations and, most importantly, not be glued to their mobile phone or be scouring the internet on their laptops. It took a little time for these ground rules to be internalized but once that happened, the meetings became more productive.

> **Pro-Tip:** Stow away your mobile phone and maintain eye contact with the speaker, especially if it is the Chair, in all meetings. You will automatically become the most acknowledged person in the room.

Working with my four Cabinet Ministers

Being Secretary to the Government of India for as long a period as four and a half years gave me the opportunity of outlasting my bosses. I had the privilege of working with as many as four Cabinet Ministers in the MDWS during my term there. Succeeding each other after relatively short tenures, they were all different, but unfailingly courteous, and soon became 'believers' in the cause.

My first Minister, when I joined on 1 March 2016, was Chaudhary Birender Singh. I had, coincidentally, met him in Dhaka a couple of months earlier at the South Asia Conference on Sanitation, when I was still the World Bank's Practice Manager for South Asia. We happened to be on the same flight while returning from Dhaka to Delhi. Sitting next to me in the business class section, he got up just before take-off, and went into the economy section of the aircraft. Soon, a lady came and sat down in his seat. It turned out that she was the minister's wife, so I went to the economy section where he was now sitting, and offered to exchange my seat with him so that he could be with his wife. He was genuinely reluctant to accept my offer but, when I insisted, gave in gracefully and went up to the business class section to sit next to his wife. Little did I know then that my 'small act of kindness' would enable me to start off on a good note when I became Secretary in his Ministry a couple of months later! When we met again on 1 March, he had become my Minister.

After a few months of my joining, Mr Singh, in a Cabinet reshuffle, left the MDWS to become the Minister for Steel, and I got a new Minister, Narendra Singh Tomar, a Member of Parliament (MP) from Gwalior in Madhya Pradesh, and an experienced grassroots politician. It was a real pleasure to work with him, and I learned a lot from him about rural communities and their main developmental challenges. Despite the multiple portfolios he held, including the Ministries of Rural Development and Panchayati Raj, Mr Tomar spent a lot of his time in advising us on how to most effectively engage with the village sarpanches* and leverage their influence to accelerate the implementation of the SBM.

My next Minister was Uma Bharti, an MP from Jhansi in Uttar Pradesh, who was previously the Minister for Water Resources, River Development and Ganga Rejuvenation. Ms Bharti was still relentlessly focused on the cleaning of the Ganga and took a lot of interest in our focused approach to making the villages along the banks of the river ODF on priority.

When the Modi government was sworn in for the second time in May 2019, I had a new Minister, my fourth, in Gajendra Singh Shekhawat. One of the younger Ministers in the new government, Mr Shekhawat, an MP from Jodhpur in Rajasthan, was dynamic and articulate. Of a new generation and very tech and social media savvy, Mr Shekhawat had travelled widely around the world, even farmed in Ethiopia, and had a solid understanding of the water-related challenges facing the country.

He was daring too, as one unforgettable episode revealed. A team of water technicians, including a Russian expert, once demonstrated an advanced 'graphene' water filter system to us. They claimed this filter could purify, to drinking water standards, the most contaminated water, which they would demonstrate in front of our eyes. As we watched, the water technicians took out a big glass jug of used engine oil and mixed in some dirt and dirty water that had been used to mop the floor. The liquid in the jug had now taken on a revolting dirty black colour. This blackish liquid was poured through the graphene filter into another glass jug. A clear, colourless and odourless liquid flowed through the filter into the second jug. The head water technician poured

---

* In most states, the village head is known as the sarpanch. In UP, however, he/she is known as the pradhan.

the clear liquid into three glasses and, while my Minister and I watched in amazement, picked up one of them and swallowed its contents in one gulp. He offered the two other glasses with the filtered liquid to us and requested us to drink as well. I hesitated, but my Minister straightaway downed the contents of the glass. I felt constrained to follow suit and drank the liquid with great reluctance. Fortunately, it tasted great – as pure water should – but I had a lingering suspicion for a few days afterwards that what I had imbibed could not have been too good for my digestive system. Luckily, I was fine.

Keeping the 'village elders' in the loop

While advising Ministers and implementing their policies was a major requirement of the job of a Secretary to the Government of India, I found it useful to keep all key players in the administration informed as well. It was critical to engage with the Cabinet Secretariat, the PM's Office (PMO), the Finance Ministry and the NITI Aayog, and get them all on board with the SBM and enlist their support. I would proactively meet them often and give them SBM progress updates, reassure them that the programme was on track to achieve its objectives, and sometimes request them to step in to send a stern message to a recalcitrant state.

I was fortunate to work closely with key seniors: the then Cabinet Secretary, P.K. Sinha, who had initiated my return to the government; the Principal Secretary to the PM, Nripendra Mishra; and the then Additional Principal Secretary to the PM, Dr P.K. Mishra, who handled all personnel matters and allowed me to select my team of senior officers. Keeping them engaged and involved in the primary aspects of the SBM not only ensured that they trusted me to work on my own terms without micro-management, but was also reassuring in that we were all on the same wavelength, in case problems arose.

Some downtime with friendly faces

I found a friend and ally in Arun Jaitley, the late Finance Minister of India. He strongly believed in the SBM and its objectives and was convinced that the programme was significantly improving the quality of life in rural India. He had a keen sense of humour and was, like myself, passionate about sports, especially tennis. Our meetings would invariably start with a discussion on a tennis topic such as which male tennis professional of our vintage had the fastest serve; we both agreed it was Roscoe Tanner. Coming to business, I would make the case for an increased budgetary allocation for the SBM given the rapid progress we were making, and he would courteously hear me out. Fortunately, the Finance Ministry, under his guidance, increased the SBM's budget significantly from year to year, based on the results achieved.

Another great supporter and friend I made during this time was Rajiv Mehrishi, the then Home Secretary and later the Comptroller and Auditor General of India. He was an outstanding civil servant with a wealth of experience and a great supporter of the SBM. He invited me a few times to address his senior Auditors General from across the country so that I could explain the objectives and modus operandi of the SBM to them. Amitabh Kant, the CEO of the NITI Aayog, was another close friend and advisor who never missed an opportunity to publicly endorse our programme. He gave valuable advice on the crucial issue of effectively engaging with the states in our federal set-up and also on using technology to closely monitor the programme. It was important for me to extend the circle of SBM believers in Delhi and I went the extra mile in getting all the key actors on board. The next big challenge, however, in our federal system of governance, lay in getting the states and districts to believe. For that, I had to become a travelling salesman.

11

The carrot is better than the stick

AS FAR BACK as 1785, the poet William Cowper had famously asserted: 'Variety is the spice of life'. With due deference to Cowper, I would venture to suggest that, in fact, competition is the (real) spice of life. Whether it is the starter's gun triggering a 100-m dash, schoolchildren competing for the highest marks in an exam, or simply a treasure hunt, competition increases the adrenaline level in most people and pushes them towards the goal. For the SBM, the goals were set: ODF villages, then districts, states and, ultimately, an ODF nation. This would be achieved by creating a people's movement, a *jan andolan*, and the key players in the nationwide competition were the state and district administrations. However, to accelerate the game's momentum, I had to take a call: was it better for us in the MDWS to dangle a carrot in front of the players or wield a stick?

In 2016, with our team having fully aligned itself with the bold vision of the PM to change the behaviour of 550 million

151

people in order to stop the practice of open defecation, I decided to revisit the PM–CM–DM (the Prime Minister–Chief Minister–District Magistrate) model to kickstart the *swachhata* engines. The PM had already articulated his vision, but in India's federal system, different states had different priorities and limited time, energy and resources to pursue those priorities. My first goal therefore was to try to make sanitation and the SBM one of the *top* priorities of all the CMs of India, to make them believe in the cause and get them committed to investing political capital, time and resources to the programme. The next goal was to get DMs excited about sanitation and have them directly champion the cause.

Becoming a travelling salesman

Marketing sanitation to the CMs and DMs was not the same as marketing roads or homes or electricity, the kind of services people usually clamour for. Toilets, or rather the lack of them, was not something that many CMs spent sleepless nights over. We were trying to market a product for which intrinsic demand didn't exist, neither from the people nor their leaders and representatives. And this made my job even more challenging, but also more exciting.

Regardless of the difficulties that lay in my path, I had the wind at my back. The SBM was a flagship programme of the PM himself. And I was viewed as a sanitation expert who had been specifically recalled to the Government of India to implement the programme. I knew I could leverage this to the SBM's advantage and engage with the states much more aggressively. And so, contrary to the traditional, more desk-bound style of working that most Secretaries to the Government of India followed, I decided to hit the road again and travel across the country on a regular basis to meet with the leadership in different states, marketing the programme personally to the CM and the Chief Secretary, the top civil servant of a state.

I would typically fly into a state capital on the morning of the meeting, call upon the CM, give him/her an update on the state's progress (or lack of it) on the programme, and compare this to the progress being made by some of the other states. Without wasting any time, I would straight away invoke my Brahmastra (the ultimate weapon, in Hindu mythology) – the fact that this was the PM's favourite programme – and would promise the CM that the Government of India was fully committed to supporting the state in its implementation of the programme. Like an itinerant medical representative trying to flog his or her medicines to a sceptical doctor, I would pull out all my cards one by one: funding, technical support, monitoring support, improvement in the quality of life of the state's rural population, and examples of other states that were making more rapid progress. In the end, I would share a road map showing how the state could achieve its goals by the stipulated deadline. I would usually find support from the Chief Secretary and we would then jointly request the CM to hold a review a week later with all DMs via videoconference. This was used to give them clear and unequivocal orders to make their districts ODF within the declared time frame. Meanwhile our team at MDWS would arrange for the funding and streamline the technical support.

I had some fascinating encounters with different CMs at various stages in my tenure. The most challenging state was always going to be UP, the most populous state in India with 230 million people, and one of the least developed in the country. UP being my home cadre in the IAS, I did have some comparative advantage and knowledge of the area. My first meeting with the then CM, Akhilesh Yadav, on a trip to Lucknow in early 2016, however, did not yield the desired results. I met him at his official residence at 5, Kalidas Marg, just opposite the Lucknow Golf Course, where I had spent many an early morning hour enjoying the game. The young CM was courteous and promised to make two districts, Kannauj and Farrukhabad, which formed part of his wife's parliamentary constituency, ODF on priority. But, as the months went by, none of the 80 districts in the state became ODF. My team and I continued to visit UP and its districts, but overall progress was slow, and the fact that the two districts mentioned by the CM were showing no signs of becoming ODF led me to conclude that the CM–DM formula was not really taking off in UP.

Fortunately, things changed in early 2017. Soon after the election to the state legislature in March 2017, a different political party – the same as the one running the Union government – took charge. I visited Lucknow and met Yogi Adityanath, the newly sworn-in Chief Minister, in the state government guest house. Clothed in saffron robes and seated on a chair covered with saffron cloth in a simply furnished room, the new CM welcomed me with a namaste. I came straight to the point: 'Sir, I need your help. UP does not have a single ODF district yet and the SBM is not doing so well in your state.' He smiled faintly and asked me what he could do to accelerate the pace of the programme. I made two suggestions for him to consider: first, appoint a dynamic young IAS officer, Vijay Kiran Anand, as the SBM Mission Director in the state and, second, publicly announce a specific number of districts in UP that would become ODF by the end of the year. Completely unfazed, he immediately agreed with my suggestions. 'We will deliver this programme and the top priority of the Hon'ble PM is now my top priority,' he said, as I left the room. The whole meeting had taken only 15 minutes. The next day the local newspapers carried the proclamation by the UP CM that 30 districts would become ODF by the end of the year and, within a few days, Vijay Kiran was appointed the Mission Director. With the weight of the CM behind the programme, the SBM began rapidly picking up pace in UP.

In the months following my meeting with the CM, the UP state government, with our support, began creating a massive army of human resources, including sanitation specialists, behaviour change experts, engineers and, most importantly, masons to build toilets. Backed with appropriate financing, no district in the state could find an excuse not to rapidly execute the CM's instructions. At the end of 2017, six districts of Uttar Pradesh had declared themselves ODF and, with the CM personally monitoring, the state began to make rapid progress.

Pro-Tip: Don't be afraid to go right to the top when required. Some deadlocks can only be resolved this way.

A few encounters with the CMs of other states were also memorable. I remember meeting Mamata Banerjee, the CM of West Bengal in Kolkata in mid-2016 to talk to her about SBM progress in her state. West Bengal was doing reasonably well and, in fact, had one of the earliest ODF-declared districts of the country: Nadia. The CM was polite and said that rural sanitation was one of her top priorities. Interestingly, the Swachh Bharat Mission was known as 'Nirmal Bangla' (Clean Bengal) in the state.

Nothing succeeds like success

While getting the CMs to buy in was imperative, it was the DMs, my penultimate clients (the ultimate being the toilet beneficiary), to whom we had to sell the programme. It was fascinating how the wheel had turned full circle: from being a DM myself many years ago, I had now returned, grey-haired, to market the SBM to a new lot of young, dynamic officers, many of whom were sceptical about my 'new and exciting' product: a toilet! And, while I had had only one or two development programmes to focus on in Bijnor, these modern-day DMs had too many programmes on their plates to implement and found it difficult to focus on any one, even if it was the CM's top priority. We had to get the DMs enthused about our programme. There were 'easy' districts and there were 'difficult' districts, and we had to motivate the DMs of both.

In the early months of my tenure, I decided to try a 'village immersion' to motivate Raman Kumar, the DM of the 'difficult' East Champaran district in Bihar (it had a sanitation coverage of less than 30 per cent) to put the SBM on top of his priority list. For this my core team and I spent two nights in a remote village to interact with the local community and understand why they were reluctant to use toilets. It was unusual, to say the least, for a Secretary to the Government of India and other senior officers to stay in the village, sleep in the local school, and wake up at dawn to observe, at a respectful distance of course, the open defecation habits of the village. Raman tried his best to persuade me to spend the nights in the comfortable circuit house, but since I insisted on staying in the village, he gave in with good grace and joined us there.

Stuck for two days with a visiting Secretary, Raman put on his creative cap to tackle the problem of rampant open defecation in his district. He decided to mobilize the schoolgirls of the district as his SBM ambassadors. He assembled them, got me to address them for effect, then eloquently persuaded them to become SBM ambassadors who would speak out against open defecation and demand toilets at home. This led to all the schoolgirls in Turkolia Block marching up and down the streets demanding household toilets. Their aggressive campaign slogan was 'Mujhe shauchalaya chahiye' (I demand a toilet) and it resulted in the SBM becoming the talk of the village communities, with a district ODF plan being prepared during our visit itself.

Apart from tackling the difficult districts, it was also imperative to demonstrate success early – at the national, state and district levels – to be taken seriously. Early success was also important to make others believe this was not an insurmountable goal after all. The best way to achieve this, I realized, was to go for the low-hanging fruit first. My team drew up a list of 60 districts which already had high sanitation coverage, and I decided to personally engage with the respective DMs to motivate them. I remembered from my time as a DM that getting a call from a Secretary to the Government of India was a pretty big deal; on top of that, a visit from this personage (like the one I had made to East Champaran) was sure to get things moving on the ground. These DMs were essentially put on overdrive with a crash course in the community approach to sanitation and encouraged to 'trigger' the villages themselves. They began creating ground-level teams to deliver behaviour change messaging at the doorstep and, often, addressed Gram Sabhas themselves. I made a WhatsApp group of the top districts and connected with all of them on a regular basis through this. I called the DMs often and visited their districts too.

By 2 October 2016, within six months of my joining, each one of these 60 districts had declared themselves ODF. They came to be viewed as islands of excellence and inspired other districts to follow suit. My team left no stone unturned to make sure the districts' success was known to everyone. We profiled the DMs on social media, got them to interact with prominent celebrities, sent them on international exposure visits, and even arranged awards for them from the PM himself. These early successes played a pivotal role in creating belief in the idea that making districts ODF was doable. It was also the first major step in our long journey towards an ODF India.

Over my four and a half years on the job, my team and I replicated this at scale. We organized many workshops where we engaged with DMs over and over again. I interacted with them in person, via videoconference from Delhi, over WhatsApp, on the phone and in every other possible way. There was no letting up. I made about 260 field visits during my tenure, met almost every CM at least once, and numerous DMs in their districts. This travelling salesman approach was a crucial part of generating and maintaining belief in the system.

Bringing in the ZSBPs

Our style of 'triggering' behaviour change, which involved evoking a sense of disgust associated with defecating in the open and that of pride about a village being ODF, was an intensive process. It began with four days of triggering and then continued with various tools and techniques. There was a sustained reiteration of the need to stop defecating in the open. While this worked seamlessly for the low-hanging fruit – the more advanced districts, sanitation-wise – the districts with lower sanitation coverage would need more ammunition and manpower.

On one of my field trips to Madhya Pradesh, while driving back to the circuit house with the DM, I saw that the young officer was a little perturbed. When I asked him what the problem was, he replied that much as he was excited about the SBM, he was being pulled in so many directions that he could not focus enough on our programme. It struck me then that we needed to provide some local support to the DMs to enable them to better implement the SBM. This led to the idea of creating a fellowship for young and talented professionals who would work in districts and be the eyes, ears and arms of the DM in implementing the SBM. We also believed that they would bring energy and a fresh perspective to the execution of the programme.

We discussed various possibilities of implementing this idea. One option was to hire the young professionals ourselves but we didn't have the capacity in government to do it fast enough. Another option was to try and create a consortium of private sector partners to loan some of their entry-level employees to be positioned in the field. I personally began reaching out to private foundations and trusts but they could not meet the demands in terms of the scale we were aiming for: one young professional per district. And so, this remained just a 'good idea', until the end of 2016, when senior members of the Tata Trusts came to my office to discuss how they could further support the SBM. It turned out to be a very fruitful meeting, where I asked them to consider taking up the entire fellowship themselves: recruit and sponsor one young professional per district in India. They had a quick consultation with their Chairman, Ratan Tata, and got back to me the next day to confirm they were on board.

A month later, on 16 December 2016, the ZSBP – Zila Swachh Bharat Prerak or District Swachh Bharat Motivator – Programme was launched jointly by Ratan Tata and our then

Minister, Narendra Singh Tomar. Over the next few months, the Tata Trusts team and ours worked together in overdrive to design the programme, invite applications, hold interviews, train the selected professionals and place them with districts in coordination with the state governments. These ZSBPs were trained, in partnership with the University of Chicago Booth School, to tackle day-to-day challenges faced in the field using behavioural and communication skills to garner the support of local officials and villagers. They were the DMs' 'point persons' for the SBM, designing training programmes and schedules for interpersonal communication with villagers to generate demand for toilets through behaviour change.

As the batches began to be deputed to the districts, in Delhi we were swamped with emails and text messages from these young activists bringing our attention to any and every issue at the village level. Even as we initially struggled to cope with and respond to these messages from the field, we welcomed the feedback from our 'boots on the ground', which pointed us towards flaws in the MIS or the SBM mobile application or highlighted gaps in sanitation coverage. Without a doubt, the Preraks played a pivotal role in infusing the SBM with focused energy and innovative ideas from the ground up.

Inspiring the young blood

In 2016, to add some zip and excitement to the budding revolution, I decided to bring in Swachh Bharat ambassador and cricket legend Sachin Tendulkar to interact with a handful of well-performing DMs and motivate them even further. When I first met Sachin at the Maurya hotel in Delhi, he was laid up in an armchair with an injured leg in a brace. Very informal and friendly, Sachin told me he would be happy to engage with

DMs but would prefer to interact with a small group rather than address a big gathering. So, we organized a small get-together in an Aerocity hotel near Delhi airport. The 25 young DMs present were thrilled to meet Sachin and bombarded him with questions in a freewheeling interaction. When one young lady asked Sachin how he brought such intense concentration to his batting, he laughed and replied he had learned to focus from his long and sometimes slow partnerships with another batting legend, Rahul Dravid. It was a spectacular evening and ended with Sachin giving each of the DMs an autographed mini cricket bat. The word spread and soon many more DMs across the country picked up their game for a chance to meet Sachin Tendulkar.

Putting them on the map

With the DM–ZSBP duo in each district motivated to tackle the ingrained behaviours head-on, we began stoking their competitive juices and made the goal of an ODF district look more and more attractive. Accelerating our social media effort, we also started putting out congratulatory posts every time a district achieved ODF status. Vineet Jain, from my front office team, came up with a great idea at this time: to literally put the competition on the map! We created a new dashboard on our MIS, open to the public, which updated itself in real time and showed progress at the national, state and district levels, literally on the map of India. This was the most powerful, live imagery of our entire journey – that map changing, district by district and state by state, from bright red (non-ODF) to bright green (ODF). Incidentally, green also happens to be my favourite colour!

The competition between districts and among states to become ODF was so intense in the first couple of years that we even had CMs enter the race. Both Kerala and Himachal Pradesh had historically high sanitation coverage and were low-hanging fruit in terms of becoming ODF states. With the objective of getting them to declare themselves ODF soon, we decided to play them against each other. I persuaded the Chief Secretary of Kerala, my IAS batchmate S. Vijayanand, to declare 1 November 2016 (Kerala Day) as his state's ODF target date. Meanwhile, I also encouraged Himachal Pradesh to also declare itself ODF soon, thinking this would happen after 1 November 2016. I had not reckoned with the competitive spirit of the Himachal Pradesh CM, though. He found out about Kerala's ODF declaration plans and landed up in Delhi in mid-October to invite our Minister, Mr Tomar, Dr J.P. Nadda, the Union Minister of Health and Family Welfare, and me to visit Simla on 30 October when the state would declare itself ODF, a day before Kerala. To clinch the deal, he even arranged for a helicopter to fly us from Chandigarh to Simla.

So, Himachal Pradesh beat Kerala to it by a day and I had to sheepishly give my batchmate the news when I visited Thiruvananthapuram the next day. A week or so later, Uttarakhand beat Haryana to the finish line by advancing its state ODF declaration event to the morning of the same day as Haryana's event, which was planned for the evening!

> **Pro-Tip:** The secret to effective management is to successfully transfer your 'worry' about achieving something to others. The person who is most worried about getting something done will always strive the hardest to achieve it.

Revving up the competition and creating an army of leaders

With more and more states and districts coming on board, it was no longer possible to focus intensely on a handful. Also, as the districts and states with already high sanitation coverage started covering the incremental gap and rapidly becoming ODF, our real challenge began: getting the districts and states with sanitation coverage of less than 30 per cent geared up to reach 100 per cent.

Employing the basic concept of competitive federalism, we began scaling up the competition between districts and states. The Swachhata Darpan initiative was launched in 2017, wherein all districts were ranked on the SBM Integrated Management Information System on key *swachhata* parameters. The competition was real, and it was online. Every day we had calls coming in from the districts with updates of progress figures. In fact, we had calls regarding our social media posts, with district ODF declarations saying: 'We uploaded our ODF certificate, where is our ODF congratulatory tweet?'

We created a core strike force of leaders among the DMs to inspire others and also act as our own personal laboratory of innovation. These young IAS officers, who were spread across the country, were brought together in a WhatsApp group: the Super 60 DMs.

One of the Super 60 DMs I remember from those early district visits was Neha Sharma in Ferozabad, UP. She had invited me to visit her district, a three-hour drive from Delhi, to study her ODF campaign. I took Amitabh Kant along with me for a World Toilet Day event there. By an interesting coincidence, all the three key players in the district were named Neha: the DM, the Chief Development Officer and the ZSBP. The DM and the other two Nehas had organized a Bal Sansad (Children's Parliament) session, where schoolkids debated and passed resolutions to make their district ODF. Amitabh and I enjoyed watching the fire and passion shown by the youngsters determined to have an ODF district soon.

Incentivizing the DMs through competition and appreciation did not stop there. Having motivated them for the cause of universal access to and usage of toilets, we also provided practical guidance and technical support to buttress their efforts. We institutionalized 'Lunch and Learn' sessions in Delhi. Every month, the team would decide a category – good performers, weak performers, districts which needed technology support, districts which were showcasing exceptional innovations – and invite the respective DMs from the district to the Ministry in Delhi for a spirited discussion with all senior officers over an organic food lunch.

The 'Lunch and Learn' idea caught on and was replicated down the line. DMs across the country began organizing their own *chai pe charcha*s (conversations over tea) with village heads and district and block coordinators. They also inspired their village motivators by participating in *ratri chaupal*s (night halts) in villages.

A fascinating development for me, now that I look back, is how many young DMs continued their interest in the SBM even after achieving ODF status for their districts. In early 2020, months after the objective of the first SBM phase had been completed, I decided to intensify my field visits and travel to the districts of states – UP, Bihar, Jharkhand and Odisha – from where we had received reports of gaps in toilet coverage. To my pleasant surprise, I was met with the same spirit as in 2016. On each of these trips, we would start the day at 5 a.m. and end at 10 p.m., and typically cover 300–400 km by night, driving across five to six districts per day. I was hugely impressed by the continued, energetic implementation of the SBM by the young DMs. They were up for the challenge, visiting every corner of their districts, conducting meeting after meeting with every block official, and making sure no one was left behind.

When I first moved to the Government of India in 1987 as Private Secretary to the Minister of State for Defence, someone asked me why I had given up the opportunity of becoming a DM in my cadre state of UP and joined the Government of India early in my career. This gentleman in Delhi, one Gulab Tiwari, said, 'The three best government jobs in India are PM, CM and DM.' Five years later, when I took up one of the three jobs, becoming the DM of Bijnor in UP, I could not agree more with Gulab Tiwari. I cannot speak for the jobs of the PM and the CM, but I can certainly confirm that there is probably no more satisfying job in India than that of a DM, the head of the district administration, who is de facto in charge of everything and everyone who moves in his or her jurisdiction, and has the raw executive power to create phenomenal change on the ground.

12

Behaviour drives people, but people can also drive behaviour

MAKING TOILETS SEXY

ALL OF US, whether at home or at the workplace, have experienced situations where we have tried, at times unsuccessfully, to persuade someone to accept an idea or a point of view. In some cases it is easy, while in others it takes much longer. It took me some time, and not a little exercise of parental authority, to convince my kids to wake up at the crack of dawn for an hour of tennis practice before they went to school. How easy, or not, was it going to be then to change the behaviour of millions of people who routinely defecated in the open? And how long would it take? Would the changed behaviour stick? We clearly had our task cut out for us if we wanted the SBM to succeed.

While marketing the SBM to the CMs and DMs was the crucial first step to mainstream the programme, this top-down approach had to be met with a corresponding 'bottom-up' one as well. This problem was too large, too complex and too long-standing to be solved by administrative writ alone.

The challenge stemmed from the simple fact that there was just no obvious demand for toilets. It was not easy to market such a product, even if it was free. As my economist wife would say, the demand for toilets was 'price inelastic'. Part of the reason for this was the deeply ingrained and centuries-old habit of open defecation. The demand for a toilet had to be stimulated to wean people away from the habit of open defecation, and therefore the behaviour change campaign had to be implemented *at scale*. Our efforts to 'trigger' at the grassroots had begun but the approach was still a little unorganized.

Harnessing the power of nudge at the grassroots – the birth of the Swachhagrahis

The SBM endeavoured to practise what Richard Thaler, the 2017 Nobel Prize-winning economist, preached on behavioural economics in his book *Nudge: Improving Decisions about Health, Wealth, and Happiness*, co-authored with Harvard Law School professor Cass Sunstein. In particular, the art of nudging: how small strategic interventions help individuals and communities change deep-seated behaviours. While the interventions were at the level of a village, given that there were more than 6,00,000 villages in the country to cover, the SBM had to undertake nudging at a scale probably unimaginable to Thaler and Sunstein.

Nudging communities to stimulate demand for toilets, and that too for 550 million people, needed a radical approach to behaviour change. After consulting numerous experts and grassroots-level practitioners, we evolved a twin strategy: ramp up interpersonal communication at the village level through trained village motivators, and, at the national level, use popular icons such as Bollywood stars and national sportspersons to promote on mass media the message of using toilets, and keep the buzz alive. For the scaling up of the former and, clearly, the more important method of behaviour change, I have to credit Pratap Bhanu Mehta, one of India's most prominent public policy intellectuals and at the time the President of the influential think tank, the Centre for Policy Research (CPR). Pratap published a regular op-ed in the *Indian Express*, a leading national daily, and was usually critical of the Union government. I had never met him, but one day got intrigued and reached out to him after reading his December 2016 op-ed where he criticized the SBM, among other flagship programmes of the government. His criticism of the SBM was mainly to the effect that we were only focused on the construction of toilets and not really trying to change behaviour.

A week later, I met Pratap at the CPR premises where we had a working lunch of idlis and dosas. Addressing his criticism, I explained that our top priority was indeed to change behaviour and stimulate demand for toilets, which then would have to be constructed. I shared our idea of using trained village-level motivators for changing behaviour and ended with: 'We're trying our best, but if you have any suggestions, we'll be happy to consider them.'

After some thought Pratap said our claim that the SBM was mainly about behaviour change would definitely be strengthened if we could credibly establish that we were developing an army of grassroots-level motivators, preferably one in each of the country's 6,00,000 villages, trained in behaviour change techniques. This, he added, would definitely give teeth to our claim, which he said currently rang rather hollow. I took his advice, and we set about creating an army of trained village motivators, who became the backbone of the programme and to whom the PM gave the brilliant name Swachhagrahi (grassroots sanitation practitioner), linking them permanently to the Mahatma's powerful term 'satyagrahi' (practitioner of truth). Today, the SBM has over 6,00,000 such swachhagrahis, an average of one per village.

Assisting the DM, like the ZSBP, the swachhagrahis were trained in the community approach to sanitation, and played a critical role in behaviour change on the ground through interpersonal communication with the village community. They used an array of context-specific 'nudge' tools and techniques, including social mapping and extensive discussion at both the community and individual household levels to convince people about the usefulness of building a toilet and then using it. In some cases, what worked was the health angle, that is, making parents, especially mothers, realize that defecating in the open meant flies would carry the excreta back to the food at home and consequently spread disease. In others, a warning to the community about the contamination of groundwater through open defecation was a strong motivator. Disgust at the shameful habit of open defecation would also be evoked. In the end, after an intense face-to-face discussion with the community, the village would be 'triggered' – the SBM's more potent proxy for 'nudged' – into accepting the fact that open defecation was not good for its people and it would consequently commit itself to becoming ODF in the shortest possible time.

Over the programme period, depending on the context, triggering took on many shapes and hues. One of the most powerful triggering methods that I witnessed first-hand in a village in UP involved a swachhagrahi bringing with her a bottle of water to share with others during a *ratri chaupal*. It was hot and dry and it had been a long day for most of the assembled people. The villagers watched intently as the swachhagrahi passed the water bottle around. Some took a sip and passed it to others, and it eventually came back to the swachhagrahi. As she continued to talk, she plucked a strand of hair off her head, bent to dip the strand into a nearby pile of cow dung, and inserted it into the water bottle. She then offered the bottle of water to the people around her. This time around, she found no takers. When she asked the villagers why they didn't want to have the water this time, they immediately responded that there was excreta in it. She then asked them if they had noticed flies sitting on their pile of excreta when they defecated in the open and then seen the same flies sit on their roti when they were eating a meal. They nodded in hushed silence. She then connected their disgust at being asked to drink from the contaminated water bottle with the image of a fly sitting on human excreta and then on their food. Surely, she stated theatrically, eating food on which the fly's six legs had deposited somebody's excreta was a definite no-no!

And so, a powerful feeling of disgust was created with respect to defecating in the open. The next time any of the assembled people saw a fly on their roti they would immediately think of the excreta carried by the fly to their roti and feel disgusted. The disgust factor would then trigger them into wanting to use a toilet instead of defecating in the open, and also motivate them to persuade others to follow suit and, finally, come together as a community to achieve ODF status for their entire village.

> **Pro-Tip:** One of the best ways to effectively communicate an idea is through powerful, emotive, imagery. It is not easy for most people to visualize a concept. Make it easy and show them what you mean.

Women comprised roughly 30–40 per cent of the swachhagrahis and played a major role in the behaviour change campaign. In some cases, they even took matters into their own hands, literally, and constructed toilets. An example of this was seen in Simdega district, Jharkhand, where women swachhagrahis stormed a traditional male bastion to become women masons, called rani mistris, and constructed a large number of toilets. Soon there were over 50,000 rani mistris in Jharkhand constructing toilets across their state. This initiative soon spread across the rest of the country.

Getting my hands 'dirty'

With the army of swachhagrahis and rani mistris storming the villages at the grassroots, we intensified our focus on changing behaviour at scale. However, somewhere around this phase, I realized that while we were moving full steam ahead on communicating for behaviour change, we had not focused enough on the product we were selling: the toilet itself. It was obviously necessary to provide the right type of toilets to those who stopped defecating in the open. Laying sewer systems in rural India was not an option due to the prohibitive cost; even urban areas in the country had less than 25 per cent coverage of networked sewer systems. The gold standard toilet technology for us was the individual household twin-pit model I had seen in

Ahmedabad within a week of taking up my new job. This toilet technology, truly 'made in India', was best suited for most rural areas in the country.

The Twin-Pit Toilet Technology

The substructure of the toilet (the part below the ground) consists broadly of two leach pits that are 1 m wide and just as deep. Above the ground is the superstructure (the toilet room) which contains a steeply sloping toilet bowl (which requires less water for flushing due to the gravity effect). Through a 'Y' junction box, the excreta is diverted into only one pit of the system, with the liquid leaching out into the earth and the solid settling down at the bottom of the pit. For a family of five, the pit usually fills up in a period of six or seven years. Once the first pit fills up, through the turn of a lever, the flow to it is stopped, and the junction box redirects the flow of excreta to the second pit. Meanwhile, in about a year, the excreta in the first pit decomposes into a greyish, odourless, powdery substance – ideal organic compost that is high in nitrogen, potassium and phosphorus content. We colloquially refer to it as *sona khaad* (golden fertilizer), and it can fetch a high price as a superb organic fertilizer for farming purposes.

But just saying that it was the 'best suited' toilet technology option wasn't going to be enough to convince everyone. I had always been a hands-on person in all my previous avatars and I wasn't going to let this one be any different. I therefore decided to walk the talk, or, rather, walk into a toilet pit and give an on-site demonstration of the efficacy of the model. I did this in a somewhat dramatic manner in February 2017, when I led my office team and a group of senior officers from all state governments to participate in a surprise toilet pit-emptying exercise in Gangadevapalli village, Warangal district, near Hyderabad city in Telangana state. Except for the state's SBM Mission Director, who was the event organizer, and a few of our core team members, no one had a clue about what would unfold. Like the pits, I had twin objectives for this exercise: first, to demonstrate the utility of the twin-pit toilet model, which produced useful organic compost out of human waste and, second, to attack the stigma associated with toilets and their emptying.

After a day's workshop in Hyderabad with senior officers from all states, we set out early next morning in buses for an innocuous enough 'field visit'. The bus was to leave at 5 a.m. sharp and, since my Delhi team of officers and consultants knew I was a stickler for punctuality, they all turned up on time. It took us about four hours to reach Warangal district and we were welcomed at Gangadevapalli village by Telangana SBM Mission Director Neetu Prasad, the Sarpanch and the rest of the community. Our busload of mostly unsuspecting passengers was then divided into five groups, with each group being led to a different site in the village.

I was led, along with my group, to a small house with a twin-pit toilet in its backyard. Within a few seconds, the circular cement cover of one of the pits was lifted and I was looking down into its almost-empty inside. Its contents looked greyish brown. The pit was deeper than I had thought and I hesitated for a second before being lowered down into it by helping hands around me. I made a soft landing, however, both literally and figuratively, on a dry cushion of human compost, while a sea of faces stared down at me. This was the first time any senior government officer had actually entered a toilet pit. A spade was handed down to me and I scooped up some compost and shovelled it into a receptacle held out for me. After a few scoops, I was lifted out of the pit and my team entered one by one and repeated my act.

Within an hour, most of the pit had been emptied and the contents placed on a blue sheet. We all scooped up some of the compost and held it out in our hands to demonstrate that it was absolutely safe to empty a pit and handle its decomposed contents, looking exactly like coffee powder, with our hands.

The impact of the toilet pit emptying was phenomenal. The *Times of India* put out a front-page story about the event the very next day, and even the PM gave it a shout-out on his monthly *Mann Ki Baat* radio address. This unique activity was a baby step towards destigmatizing the emptying of a toilet pit. Soon well-known personalities, including Mr Rajiv Mehrishi, the Comptroller and Auditor General of India, Amitabh Kant, CEO of the NITI Aayog, and Akshay Kumar, the Bollywood actor, joined us in emptying toilet pits in different states, which gave a significant boost to the programme.

The Gangadevapalli toilet pit-emptying event was an important milestone in the SBM journey – it led to the promotion of the twin-pit toilet model and also attacked the conventional stigma associated with cleaning toilets.

Pro-Tip: Don't ask others to do something you wouldn't do yourself. Do it yourself first, and others will follow.

Beyond the mandate and some small-screen affairs

With the ground game gaining momentum, I set forth to make the SBM more widespread, to take the sanitation conversation from a solely rural context to making it 'everyone's business'. As a true *swachhata* campaigner, I began to hold one-on-one meetings with other Secretaries to the Government of India and potential stakeholders to adopt safe sanitation as a primary objective in their respective sectors. I made such a nuisance of myself that most Secretaries, just to keep me out of their hair, did as I asked. The result was that *swachhata* was everywhere, and it was there to stay. The most striking example of this was the addition of SBM's iconic logo – Gandhiji's glasses – on all Indian currency notes.

I began engaging with celebrities regularly to keep the buzz going. Thus was born the Darwaza Band campaign with the great Amitabh Bachchan and the popular Anushka Sharma. Early in my tenure, I requested the megastar to do a short film for us to promote the cause of ending open defecation and using toilets instead. The World Bank supported us by hiring the advertisement agency Lowe Lintas to direct the SBM film featuring the two celebrities. The theme, finally agreed upon after hours of discussions with the Lintas team, was to get the duo to exhort their fellow villagers to 'shut the door' (Darwaza Band) on open defecation.

As the programme completed Phase-I of its implementation of an ODF India in 2019, even the National Geographic channel aired a documentary film about how the SBM was being implemented at the grassroots and how it was harnessing the power of a huge population to bring about substantial and sustainable change in the centuries-old habit of defecating in the open. The documentary premiered on 8 March 2020, International Women's Day, with a special screening for the President of India at Rashtrapati Bhawan.

On the red carpet with Akshay Kumar

In mid-2016, I had the opportunity to meet Bollywood superstar Akshay Kumar. Inspired by the SBM, Akshay was thinking of producing and acting in the first ever commercial film on toilets which, in true Bollywood style, was to be called *Toilet – Ek Prem Katha** (*TEPK*). Through my old friend Datta Padsalgikar, the then Mumbai Commissioner of Police, I managed to meet with the star at the film's outdoor shoot in Mathura towards the end of December 2016. I found Akshay and his co-star, a new actress at the time called Bhumi Pednekar, playing cards in a small house, which was the main movie set. We discussed the script of the movie, which was loosely based on classic Bollywood storylines: boy meets girl, they fall in love and get married. Girl, who comes from a home which has a toilet, finds that her new home doesn't have one and that she has to go outside to defecate along with the other women of the village. She protests and leaves him. He woos her back by building a toilet at home despite his father's vehement protests. It ends with them living happily ever after. Clearly, this movie would

---

* Toilet – A Love Story

help us with our message of behaviour change, and Akshay and I decided to keep in touch for edits and inputs as the shooting progressed.

In November 2016, following up from that initial meeting in Mathura, Akshay invited our team to Mumbai for a viewing of the first cut of the film. While I am an early riser, my usually late-rising team was shattered to be told the viewing was scheduled for 5 a.m. at a film studio near Juhu Beach. I first went to Akshay's house, a large mansion on the beach, at 4.30 a.m. and found him in a track suit, having just completed his workout. He offered me a glass of thick, glutinous and unappetizing-looking papaya juice. Wishing I had a designated drinker on this occasion too – as during my visit to Kunming as part of the World Bank's China programme – I somehow gulped it down while Akshay looked on approvingly, before we left for the film studio.

As the film started, we straight away spotted some issues. Later, with Akshay being gracious enough to ask for our feedback, I suggested three changes in the script: first, that the hero should build a twin-pit toilet for his bride and not a massive septic tank toilet; second, that the hero should refuse the government grant for the toilet and say he would like to pay for it himself out of love for his wife; and third, that the 'toilet scam' scene in the movie should be scrapped. The 'toilet scam' was that of a government servant not doing his job and instead indulging in corrupt practices. While Akshay agreed with my first two suggestions, he politely disagreed with the third. 'Come on, Mr Iyer,' he said, 'every Bollywood movie has a scam. I need to have at least some *masala* (spice) in my film for it to sell.' As it turned out, *TEPK* was a blockbuster commercial hit and we also used it extensively as a behaviour change communication tool.

At the end of the film screening, at around 8 a.m., Akshay treated all of us to a sumptuous breakfast of omelettes, idlis, dosas and chole bhature. Throughout my association with him, including his occasional visits to my home in Delhi, he has been a spartan eater, but this time he tucked in with the rest of us. As for me, I enjoyed the delicious, greasy food after having to stomach the nutritious papaya juice in the early hours of the morning.

Flushing me down the toilet

As the Secretary MDWS cum de facto Mission Director of this national flagship programme, I had to act as a spokesperson for the SBM-G, make media appearances on TV panel discussions and join the Minister at press conferences. It was useful to be in front of the cameras and share the Swachh Bharat story 'straight from the horse's mouth' as it were. I made some great friends during this period, especially the incomparable Shekhar Gupta and the two high-calibre India Today TV anchors, Rajdeep Sardesai and Rahul Kanwal. I remember being a little apprehensive before the first of my *Off the Cuff* panel discussions with Shekhar, but he put me at ease before asking the inevitable tough questions in his own gentle way. Other mediapersons I actively engaged with included Tavleen Singh, with whom I had a breakfast meeting series going, and T.N. Ninan, who gave me blunt feedback.

It was also during this time that I began my friendship with Raj Chengappa, Editorial Director of the *India Today* news magazine, one of the top English news magazines in the country. I met Raj early in my tenure as Secretary, MDWS, when he came to meet me regarding sanitation efforts in the country. At that point, *India Today* had already been doing a fine job itself of publicly recognizing the good work being done on sanitation through its 'Safaigiri' initiative. Although Raj was keen to send his team to the field to do an 'SBM in action' feature, somehow this never did materialize over the years. Towards the end of 2019, Raj called me to do an interview for a special edition magazine the India Today group was preparing: their annual 'Unsung Heroes of the Year'.

The interview itself was business as usual. We sat together for a while and had an informal chat about the programme and, to complete the process, I met Bandeep Singh, the photo editor, in his studio in Noida for some pictures to accompany the piece. When the edition came out, to my horror, I saw they had put me on the cover. Now, while that might not sound like a dire situation, the cover picture was that of me relaxing nonchalantly *inside* a toilet bowl!

While the congratulations from family, friends and colleagues poured in, I have to confess I was a little flustered thinking about the reaction from the higher-ups. I was curious about whether the PM would have seen this offbeat picture and, to be honest, a little apprehensive about his views on it. To Indira's and my great relief, the PM freed us of our tension at the Army Day reception line-up on 10 January 2020 – seeing Raj Chengappa standing next to us, the PM gave a broad smile and told him, while pointing at me: '*Aapne toh inko toilet mein dooba diya!*' (You flushed him down the toilet!)

From local lavatory to global laboratory

With the topic of sanitation finding its way even into social gatherings, we found it useful to keep the buzz alive at the national level. This strengthened not only the marketing of our hitherto unsung product, the toilet, but also the will and resolve of all those working for the cause.

In October 2018, to celebrate the annual Swachh Bharat Diwas and take our learnings to the world, we organized the Mahatma Gandhi International Sanitation Convention (MGISC). What began as just an idea during a routine office meeting in March 2018 became a three-day global event in the run-up to 2 October 2018, with a line-up of plenary addresses, panel discussions and even a field trip to a village in Gujarat. The first MGISC ended up being nothing short of spectacular. Over 200 delegates from across the world joined the event with 55 Ministers in charge of sanitation also in attendance.

There were a few tense moments during the event, especially at midnight on 1 October, when we struggled to find the appropriate location for the group photograph of the high dignitaries attending the concluding session the next morning. Luckily, I noticed a huge portrait of Mahatma Gandhi in a large room adjacent to the main convention hall and we made that the spot. The group photograph turned out very well, with the painting of the person who had inspired the SBM in the backdrop, and PM Modi and UN Secretary-General Antonio Guterres in the middle of the assembled Ministers.

It was at this convention that the Delhi Declaration was signed by the PM, the UN Secretary-General, and visiting Ministers from all participating nations. The Delhi Declaration articulated the four pillars for any successful large-scale

behaviour change programme as employed by the SBM: the 4
Ps – Political Leadership, Public Financing, Partnerships and
People's Participation.

I still get a laugh out of how, at the end of the MGISC, my
good friend Val Curtis turned to me and said, 'Congratulations,
Param, you just made sanitation sexy.'

13

If your boss is on board, go to town

LEVERAGING THE PM'S LEADERSHIP

IN OUR PROFESSIONAL lives, we all have somebody we report to, or someone we find ourselves answerable to. It could be your immediate boss, a senior colleague or even a client. What many of us forget, however, is that the boss is not just someone who supervises your work; the boss can also be leveraged to maximize your output and help you to achieve your objectives. If your boss believes in what you're doing, don't hesitate to use his or her influence to get things moving.

In my case, although the Minister was my immediate superior, I was, in a sense, answerable for the delivery of the SBM to the Big Boss himself: the Prime Minister of India. While serving in the IAS, the closest I had ever come to a direct connect with a PM was in Dehradun in 1984, when, as SDM, I had done a namaste to Mrs Gandhi. As Secretary to the Government of India, however, I now had direct access to the PM. Not only was I senior enough to request a meeting with him, I was also privileged to have been handed the responsibility of delivering one of his highest priority flagship projects. The deck was clear to leverage the full might of the PM's leadership to achieve the SBM's goal.

Leveraging the leader

As a manager, one is entrusted with a leadership role. One typically oversees the work of a group of employees and is responsible for delivering a task. In most of my previous jobs as a manager, while I would seek the guidance of my boss from time to time, I had never thought of making a conscious effort to use him or her to make my task *easier*. As the Secretary, MDWS, however, and tasked with a mission as gigantic as making the country ODF, I would have been a fool not to leverage the PM's immense popularity and clout as well as his willingness to invest his political capital in the SBM.

I took full advantage of the leverage afforded to me. So much so, that a few years into the implementation of the programme, with many an SBM 'PM event' under our belt, a top official in the PMO said to me: 'No other Secretary to the Government has utilized the PM's mass appeal for a flagship programme as much you have.'

In PM Modi's case, there were several, more substantive, reasons to leverage the leader. Apart from providing the big vision and lending his political weight to supporting the SBM, many of the key initiatives, ideas and symbols associated with the programme came directly from him. The selection of Mahatma Gandhi's reading glasses as the crowdsourced logo of the SBM and its tag line – '*Ek kadam swachhata ki ore*' (One step towards cleanliness) was a masterstroke – as was the idea of making the programme a people's movement, a *jan andolan*, and the launch of the Swachhata Hi Seva campaigns. Terms and phrases that rolled off one's tongue, such as swachhagrahi and 'Satyagraha se swachhagraha tak' (From striving for truth to striving for sanitation), also came from him.

The architect of the SBM, the PM, continually contributed ideas and strategies with respect to the programme. He gave me two such ideas at my first meeting with him on 30 April 2016. After listening patiently to my proposed strategy, he suggested that we prioritize the villages along the Ganga river for ODF status and also select 100 iconic places of tourist interest across the country and clean up their surroundings to international standards. From then onwards, I sought meetings with him regularly – to keep him apprised of what was going on and seek his guidance.

The Communicator-in-Chief

Wherever you work, once a policy decision has been taken and a vision articulated, it is key to align yourself to the vision of your leader. It is also important to fully understand and be clear about the priorities underpinning the vision. I realized from the beginning that the PM's key interest lay in actively involving the people of the country in the SBM: getting them to own and lead the programme at the grassroots level, and making the SBM a true *jan andolan* and not just a *sarkari* programme.

A charismatic orator and a superb communicator, PM Modi was our trump card in the campaign, and we strategically used him as our Communicator-in-Chief, whether it was to appeal to the nation to join the revolution and lead the charge for *swachhata*, or to address key stakeholders – our grassroots force – to encourage them in this effort for a Swachh Bharat.

The PM's monthly *Mann Ki Baat* (MKB) radio address became an incubator of ideas for us, and on no occasion did we miss giving the PMO a *swachhata* input for it. In total, the PM spoke of *swachhata* in 47 of the 65 MKB addresses he had made as of May 2020. This made the SBM the most promoted scheme on the PM's programme on All India Radio, which has an over 90 per cent penetration in the country.

We would use the PM's MKB programme to maximum effect, sometimes leveraging his spoken word to endorse our proposals. One of the most effective endorsements we got from his MKBs was for the ZSBP programme, where he said the following: 'The Government of India has also appealed to the corporate world to come forward in this endeavour. They can sponsor young professionals willing to work for the *swachhata* mission. They can also be sent to various districts as Swachh Bharat Fellows.'

The Tata Trusts' sponsorship of the ZSBP programme soon followed. A few other initiatives that sprang from the PM's MKB addresses were the Swachh Bharat Summer Internship and the Swachh Sundar Shauchalaya (Clean and Beautiful Toilet) – a campaign wherein over 10 million toilets were decorated and painted in a month's time as households took pride in their *izzat ghar* (house of pride).

Pro-Tip: If you have an idea you believe in, propose it, even if it seems outlandish. Bosses are usually on the lookout for initiative and new proposals.

Chalo Champaran

By mid-March 2018, we were making steady progress under the SBM with rural sanitation coverage at 84 per cent and 15 states and union territories having already declared their rural areas ODF. We were getting closer to the goal but were behind in some states – Bihar, UP, Odisha and Jammu & Kashmir.

To encourage Bihar to accelerate implementation of the SBM, I put up a proposal to the PMO for the PM to consider addressing a large rally of Swachhagrahis at Champaran in Bihar on 10 April – the same site where, 101 years ago, Mahatma Gandhi had launched the Champaran agitation against the British colonial masters. The PM agreed and we took the opportunity to 'trigger' the entire state of Bihar by unleashing 20,000 Swachhagrahis –10,000 from Bihar and 10,000 from all over the country – across the state for a full week prior to the 10 April event, touching every village in every district in the state. It was a BHAG of its own, a 'wild' idea but definitely worth trying. Given how dear sanitation was to Gandhiji, the campaign was named 'Satyagraha se Swachhagraha Tak' and marked the culmination of the centenary celebrations of the Champaran Satyagraha agitation.

Prior to the upcoming Champaran event, the PM chaired a videoconference with the DMs of the four lagging states, including Bihar of course, and set specific targets for behaviour change and toilet construction during the three-week period culminating on 10 April. The stiffest target was set for Bihar, with a total of 1 million toilets to be constructed during this period. At the videoconference, the PM was at his charismatic best, inspiring the young DMs, especially those of Bihar, to rise to the occasion and achieve the specific, time-bound targets he had set for them. This direct PM–DM connection worked like a charm and generated incredible momentum in the run-up to the event.

After a few weeks of intense coordination and logistics planning, the swachhagrahis from across the country started arriving in Bihar in the first week of April 2018. Soon, reports started flying in from village after village of Bihari swachhagrahis working with those from outside the state, meeting community after community and discussing the importance of sanitation. Language barriers were broken, with Tamil-speaking swachhagrahis or those from the North-east partnering with Hindi-speaking counterparts from the state to trigger villages. Cross-country cultural exchanges never witnessed before occurred that week, reconfirming the country's unity in diversity. It was one week of pure concentrated revolution as, literally, the entire country came together to give Bihar a helping hand.

At the mega event in Motihari, Champaran, on 10 April, the PM addressed a charged-up audience of 20,000 swachhagrahis, full of excitement after having successfully 'triggered' Bihar. It was a surreal day. To begin with, some political parties called for a Bharat Bandh (country-wide shutdown) that day due to which most of the roads were blocked and the movement of cars disrupted. To add to the confusion, our compère for the PM's event did not reach the venue on time and we had to manage with a last-minute substitute. Luckily, everything went off like clockwork, with even the looming thunderstorm holding off till the event ended.

A pleasant surprise

There was an unexpected moment coming for me during the event. I received the PM at the mini exhibition of *swachhata raths* (sanitation chariots) outside the huge tent under which the massive audience was assembled, and accompanied him as he walked around, having a few words with each of the swachhagrahis we had selected from different parts of the country. Having completed the round, he left for his 'green room' where he would spend a few minutes before being invited to join the other dignitaries on the dais. Meanwhile, I took my seat among the audience. In my experience of organizing many a PM–SBM public event, this was the time when I could relax a bit: from this time onward till the PM departed, my role was limited to listening to the addresses by the PM and the Ministers.

By the time the PM's address started, the exhaustion after the intense days and nights of the Champaran preparation had begun to catch up with me. A little distracted, I was suddenly elbowed by Anjani Singh, my IAS batchmate and Chief Secretary of Bihar, who was sitting on my right. 'Sit up, man,' he hissed. 'The PM is talking about you.' He was right and I was stunned. The PM had deviated from his main speech and was speaking about me warmly, about how I had given up the good life in the US and returned to India to implement the SBM. He also directed the TV cameraman to focus the camera upon me so that the audience could see me on the huge LED screens. Almost in a daze, I rose to my feet and did a namaste to the smiling PM. Going on for a few minutes, the PM ended his reference to me with: 'If, like Parameswaranji, all of you assembled swachhagrahis could work with us on our Swachh Bharat Mission, we will definitely succeed in achieving our goal.'

While I was humbled by the PM's gracious words, I was also aware that such praise might evoke resentment among some of my fellow civil servants. On conferring with Indira, she agreed and bluntly told me 'to lie very low'. It was sound advice from her, as always, and I tried my best to follow it after the Champaran event.

> **Pro-Tip:** There is no such thing as Mission Accomplished. Achieving a milestone is important but it is equally important to get up the next morning and saddle up for the next.

Go to town!

The Champaran event led to the expected acceleration in rural sanitation coverage in Bihar, but there was another positive spin-off. After Champaran, the state governments took SBM implementation even more seriously than before. This enhanced the effectiveness of my travelling salesman role, especially in marketing the SBM to the remaining, more difficult, states.

As time went by, we continued to leverage the PM's mass appeal for programmatic purposes. In the four-plus years that I worked on the SBM, we ended up doing a record 10 major public events with the PM, something no other national flagship programme has come even close to achieving.

At the beginning of 2019 , we already had two PM events with our grassroots force scheduled for the year. The first was *Swachh Shakti*, in Kurukshetra, honouring the grassroots women leaders of the SBM. The second was the historic *Swachh Kumbh Swachh Aabhar* event where the PM debunked the arbitrary caste distinctions drawn by society and felicitated sanitation workers at the *Kumbh Mela*, taking everyone by surprise when he washed the feet of five sanitation workers to express the nation's gratitude for their service.

If I could express in writing what happened backstage and describe the energy in the hall when the video of the PM washing the workers' feet reached the 10,000 participants from the Kumbh Mela, I would. But since I cannot, you will just have to take my word for it: it was surreal, standing outside the closely guarded room where the PM and the sanitation workers were. The one thing I can reveal is the attention to detail paid by the PM. He conveyed a message to me before the event that I should make sure the water in the brass bucket to be used for washing the feet was lukewarm and not freezing cold (it was a wintry February afternoon).

There are moments in life when one is overwhelmed by the magnitude of human empathy. For me, standing outside the closely guarded room where the PM was washing the feet of the sanitation workers, that was one such moment.

The personal touch

In addition to the one-on-one meetings I had with the PM, my family members were also privileged to have met him over the course of my years on the job. Indira met him on four or five occasions, usually at evening receptions at the Rashtrapati Bhawan on the occasion of India's Independence Day, Republic Day or Civil Services Day. The PM, with his great sense of humour, would invariably come up with a quip when he spoke to her. The first time he met her while we were standing in the line-up to welcome him, he returned her namaste and, pointing at me, said to her with a smile: '*Kya aap ne inko ghar pe swachhata par lagaya hai*?' (Have you put him on cleaning activities at home?) Indira was always thrilled to meet him, and was really inspired by the PM's development vision at her last interaction with him at 7, Lok Kalyan Marg, on 20 August 2020 when we met him together for a farewell meeting.

My 91-year-old father, Air Marshal P.V. Iyer (retired), a great admirer of PM Modi, was also very keen to meet him. This finally happened on 8 October 2018, during the Air Force Day reception at the Air House, residence of the Chief of the Air Staff. My father and I had been invited for the reception and, among the thronging military crowd of Air Marshals, Generals and Admirals, we met Hardeep Puri, the Minister of Civil Aviation and of Urban Development. I introduced my father to the Minister and mentioned that he was hoping for a chance to shake hands with the PM. However, the PM did not come near my father while being steered around the reception area. Disappointed, we were about to leave when, suddenly, the host, Air Chief Marshal S.S. Dhanoa, made an announcement: 'Air Marshal Iyer is requested to come up to meet the Hon'ble PM.' Minister Puri had done the trick, requesting the PM to meet my father. I followed my dad as he walked up to greet the PM, who shook hands with him and, extremely graciously, spent a few minutes talking to him about his service career. My dad was thrilled and when we returned home, immediately opened up a new bottle of single malt Scotch whisky and had a couple of quick ones to celebrate his encounter with the PM.

My daughter Tara, also a big fan of the PM, was very keen to meet him before she left to join her job as an economist at the International Monetary Fund in Washington DC in September 2019. The PM was kind enough to give her an appointment and Tara and I went to his residential office. I was a silent participant as he enthusiastically engaged with her, asking about her tennis-playing career and listening patiently to her ideas on the Indian economy. As we left, the PM wished Tara all the best in her new job and told her to feel free to send him emails from Washington DC with any interesting ideas she had on the global or the Indian economy.

It has been a fascinating experience to have had the opportunity for several one-on-ones with PM Modi. I never left a meeting with him without having a novel idea to pursue or some new food for thought. He is always patient in listening, regardless of whether he is about to agree or disagree with somebody. He thinks big and outside the box. But what resonates the most with me is that he keeps a relentless focus on the last-mile delivery of development programmes, which, I think, is one of the most critical factors required for India to move ahead on its development path.

14

Look outside the echo chamber

YOU MAY IMAGINE that a CEO's or a manager's fantasy would be an organization or team where everyone agrees with each other. A workplace where the staff blindly follows the leader, and where there is no disagreement of opinion, may appear to be ideal but, believe me, it isn't. In fact, if you are ever in such a situation, you need to opt for a major rejig in the workplace. Having a few naysayers in the team, or outside the team, who ask questions – even awkward ones sometimes – is actually akin to having a safety valve because the 'boss is always right' syndrome can be dangerous. If these people don't already exist in your ecosystem, you would do well to find someone who can play this role. I was fortunate in my job as Secretary, MDWS, that I had such people both inside and outside the organization.

My in-house conscience keeper – my spouse, Indira

I have been very fortunate that my wife, Indira, has been my best friend and toughest critic throughout my career. Although a wholehearted supporter, she has never minced words when it comes to expressing her opinion. Even after our return to Delhi, with a hectic job herself in the Ministry of Finance – as the Chief Director of Research in the Tax Policy and Research Unit – she was always available for advice and in fact instrumental in bringing some method into the madness of my varied career.

As far back as my Swajal days, she would remind me to take a step back and take the pressure off my officers when we were charging ahead to achieve a specific time-bound objective. Her advice was always context-specific: and when I took up the job of Secretary, Indira was the one who told me that since I then had only a two-year contract, I needed to make every day count. She suggested it would be useful to mark off, on a whiteboard in my office, the number of days I had spent on the job and those that were left. Her 'tough love' advice was very helpful when it came to listening to and engaging with our critics – and we had plenty of them.

T.N. Ninan, one of the most senior and respected economic journalists in the country, was one such early critic. Like some others, he was of the opinion that we were on a toilet-building spree and were neglecting the crucial behaviour change element of the SBM. Indira suggested that I reach out to him: 'You can at least tell him about your programme's efforts at behaviour change and seek his advice.' So, I contacted Mr Ninan and we met for coffee at a 'neutral' venue. While he started out being quite critical about the programme, I was at least partially successful in impressing upon him that we were trying hard to change behaviour but the scale of the problem was obviously a challenge. His blunt, very Ninan-like advice was for us to reach out more proactively to people outside the government and clearly communicate the SBM's behaviour change strategy. It was a very useful meeting and served two purposes. First, Mr Ninan understood – and hopefully appreciated – what we were trying to achieve. And, second, we began ramping up our communication strategy to the outside world.

Witness to the MPs – and the college connection

On the core programme front, I didn't have to look too far outside the echo chamber to get some even more 'objective' feedback about my job. I found myself quite literally at the receiving end within only a couple of weeks of taking up my new job in March 2016. An integral part of the job of Secretary to the Government of India is to represent one's Ministry as a 'witness' at a Parliamentary Committee hearing a few times a year. This can be a harrowing experience, as the Hon'ble MPs are usually blunt and critical about the working of Ministries and do not hold back on asking tough questions of the 'witness': the Secretary. I would have preferred to have a little more time to get used to the job, but I had little choice in the matter and was summoned in mid-March before the MDWS's Parliamentary Standing Committee to discuss the 2016–17 budget proposal. Waiting apprehensively outside the Witness Room in the Parliamentary Annexe building, I was introduced to Kirti Azad, MP from Bihar and a member of the Parliamentary Committee. He had been an outstanding cricketer and member of the Indian team which won the 1983 World Cup. He was also from my college: St. Stephen's. We exchanged pleasantries before he moved on to join the other MPs inside the Witness Room. After he left, one of my officers whispered to me that Mr Azad was one of the toughest and most aggressive interrogators on the Parliamentary Committee. I fervently hoped our college connection would soften his approach.

A few minutes later, I was summoned inside and ushered to the witness seat. After making a detailed presentation on the SBM and our rural drinking water programme and the broad implementation strategy going forward, I was bombarded with critical questions and comments by the MPs. Most of them pertained to implementation gaps on the ground in their respective constituencies. I attempted to respond to each of their questions and, despite my relative inexperience, it seemed that my belief in the SBM and willingness to take advice from the MPs had come through. Even Mr Azad seemed relatively non-combative in his questioning. Maybe the college connection had worked after all.

As I came out of the hearing, I realized I had received useful and constructive feedback from the MPs, who knew and understood the ground reality of such programmes better than most of us. In fact, their early input was an important factor in making me determined to understand the ground reality myself by travelling extensively to the field and interacting with the beneficiaries of our programmes.

Grey hair and young blood – a winning combination

Those familiar with the government set-up would know that the department I headed came with a list of officers, specialists and consultants – each equipped with their own skills and, in many cases, years of experience. The team in the Secretary's personal office, or the front office team, however, as I have mentioned earlier, consisted of three young professionals from the Tata Trusts with barely any experience. Two of the three, Mahima

Vashisht and Vineet Jain, joined my office right at the beginning, while the third, Karishma Kadyan, came in a year and a half later.

My front office team had limited background in the sanitation sector, and no experience at all of working in large governmental set-ups. This turned out to be an advantage in terms of their playing the role of sounding board within the organization. Like my informal interaction with Minister Arun Singh when I was his Private Secretary many years ago, the engagement with my front office team was more informal than it was with the official hierarchy of the MDWS. For example, I could easily draw upon tennis analogies while strategizing for the plan of action to nudge tough districts to become ODF, while they could present more radical views as we prepared a communication strategy for behaviour change. A lot of these ideas would then correctly be challenged by the senior officers, and we almost always arrived at a consensus. It was also a great help to have a high-energy, creative team that could, after a short discussion with me, convert the agreed ideas into high-quality, impactful PowerPoint presentations and other resource material for my use at short notice. They also played a key role in helping us build the SBM brand and increase our media presence, especially on social media.

The front office team was bright, articulate, analytical and positive, and also displayed very good interpersonal skills in getting along with the senior officers without ruffling too many feathers.

Pro-Tip: Encourage innovation even if it flouts hierarchy. An idea can emerge from anywhere or anybody.

Development partners

Others outside the MDWS whom I regularly consulted as the programme progressed included external agencies such as UNICEF, the World Bank and the Bill and Melinda Gates Foundation (BMGF), all of which became staunch allies of the SBM. They were all ready to provide support, bring in international experts to assist and advise us when necessary, and extend a helping hand to us in the march towards the SBM goal. The development partners were available to counsel and refresh our priorities as the need arose. They were involved in strategic discussions, and provided support on the ground and even communication material time and again.

Leveraging their role of honest broker, we would sometimes also use the development partners as intermediaries to engage with some of the naysayers, and explain to them how we were trying to roll out the largest behaviour change programme in the world and what hurdles we were facing.

Keep your friends close and your enemies closer

Direct outreach to our harshest critics, however, was important and we ourselves reached out to an assorted group of foes of the SBM, organizing the Swachh Bharat Dialogues with hard-boiled journalists and critical researchers from leading institutions across the country.

I would like to be able to report to you that the Dialogues went off very well and that we 'converted' our critics into 'true believers', but the truth is that we were only partially successful. The Dialogues did result in us getting plenty of suggestions, some of which we accepted, but a large part of the advice was academic and came from people who did not understand the challenges of implementing programmes on the ground. The 'glass-half-empty walas' seemed to be an apt descriptor for them.

But the Dialogues did introduce us to some people who gave us great constructive advice, such as Dr N.C. Saxena, the highly regarded former civil servant and development expert. Not a person to mince words, he pointed out the problem of the pre-SBM single-pit toilets but also proposed the solution: retrofitting them by adding a second pit to ensure that the toilet need not be shut down after the single pit filled up. This was sound advice, which we duly followed.

Think laterally

As mentioned, reaching out laterally to people 'outside the system' was one of the main ways I attempted to look beyond the echo chamber. Ironically, I myself was a lateral entrant into the government, having technically come in as Secretary to the Government of India from the outside. In addition to mine, the government made a few more senior lateral appointments. A few of these 'outsider' appointments led to some resentment among the IAS officers. In my own case, however, I have to admit that, after some initial hesitation, my former IAS colleagues warmly welcomed me back to the fold. Personally, I am convinced that it is useful to bring in new ideas and energy from 'outside' the system and marry these with the experience and understanding of the 'insiders'. The Modi government deserves credit for accelerating this process in recent years.

As far as the 'permanent' insiders are concerned, as I have mentioned earlier, I believe that in this day and age of specialized skills and domain knowledge, it is important for the IAS to re-engineer itself and encourage officers, after about 15 years of field experience, to 'specialize' in certain broad areas such as the social sector, infrastructure, environment and energy, finance and economics, and so on. The selection process for officers at the highest levels in the Government of India should also be made more targeted, and, I believe, based on inviting applications and holding interviews to find the best fit for the job.

Live a little

While working on the SBM itself was exhilarating for most of us, I decided to occasionally introduce some fun in the workplace, as I had in most of my previous jobs. In my view people will only give their best when they are enjoying what they are doing. It is therefore useful to go beyond the professional and bring in some exuberance and joy to your working environment. For many of us, the hours we spent at the office were sometimes double the time we spent at home with our families, and it would have been a pity if we hadn't mixed a little enjoyment with those long office hours!

During my time at the MDWS, I organized a number of 'retreats' for our entire SBM team. We would usually invite the state SBM Secretaries and Mission Directors for these. We would also often invite champion DMs from across the country to give us ground-level feedback about the programme. To attract as many participants as possible, we would also try to hold these retreats at interesting venues outside Delhi. I would usually get hold of an interesting, out-of-the-box speaker who could hold the attention of the audience. Our first such retreat was held at Udaipur, Rajasthan, where I invited Professor Val Curtis to come and talk to us about the science of disgust and how it could help influence behaviour change. Among other charismatic speakers at different events, we got Shiv Khera, the motivational guru, to inspire our team to greater heights at Mathura; Kiran Bedi, the first woman Indian Police Service officer in India, to charge up a group of state and district officials at Hyderabad; and of course superstars Akshay Kumar and Aamir Khan to interact with our star-struck young DMs. My only regret is that we never managed to execute the oft-discussed plan to hold a retreat at that venue of venues: Goa!

After mega events and unusually stressful work weeks, Indira and I would host the larger team for get-togethers at home, with games and entertainment as well as creative mock awards and certificates for each member of the MDWS family. The first time we did this, my team gave me the title 'POTUS' which was a dig at my propensity to call them to the office on weekends: it stood for 'Postponement of Topic Until Saturday'! The next year, I was given the title 'Mr CLTS' – 'Mr Collectively Let Them Suffer', a pun on the Community-Led Total Sanitation technique. To the team's credit, they tried to make up for all the jabs with a flattering certificate at the last such gathering, which said 'Mr Super @ 60' since I had just turned 60. The play was on our WhatsApp group of Super 60 DMs.

All work and no play...

To really switch off work, apart from the rare and brief holidays I took with Indira, with Tara and Venkat occasionally joining, I made it a point to join some very good friends for a round of golf a couple of times a week. I used to be addicted to the game many years ago, before my kids took up tennis, and coming back to Delhi in March 2016 was an opportunity to pick it up again. I have to confess, though, that I was initially a little shaky about admitting to anyone that I played golf, thinking that this 'elitist' pursuit of sporting pleasure would not mix well with the strict and austere work ethic propagated by the government. I soon found out, however, that many senior civil servants, including those who worked in the most important offices, played golf regularly. After my initial hesitation, I took the plunge and admitted to one of the most senior civil servants in the country at a dinner party that I too was a golfer. He immediately roped me into his group and, throwing caution to the winds, I became a golfer again after almost 25 years!

I would usually team up with Rajiv Mehrishi, Amitabh Kant, and K.P. Krishnan, Secretary, Ministry of Skill Development, for some early morning golf at the Delhi Golf Club, before reaching office at 8.30 a.m. Although it was mostly to do with pure pleasure, the 5.30 a.m. golf round turned out to be a great time for us to 'talk shop', when we exchanged thoughts and ideas about work and, of course, caught up with the usual civil services gossip. Both Rajiv Mehrishi and Amitabh Kant were also on hand when we celebrated my father's ninetieth birthday at home by breaking open a bottle of Blue Label. While I toasted my dad with my staple nimbu-pani, the two of them joined him in a more conventional toast.

Pro-Tip: Develop a hobby or an interest outside of your work. You will be more effective at your job if you can switch off from the office when you leave it.

I will reiterate that it is always useful to have some people around you who will dispassionately call a spade a spade. It is easy to get carried away and drawn into a mental model of believing that one can do no wrong, especially when one is in a position of power or influence. But looking outside the echo chamber or, better still, bringing in some contrary views *into* the echo chamber, will help you take balanced and well-thought-out decisions.

15

Go on the front foot when required

THERE WILL ALWAYS be times when, no matter how hard you try or how well you do, some people will just not be pleased with your efforts. While it is wise to try to take their criticism on board and improve your work further, there will be times when you realize they are being critical just for the sake of being critical – these are the non-constructive type of critics. Such critics are best ignored, for the most part. But remember, 'man bites dog' is always the more interesting story, and if these non-constructive critics persist, they will garner attention. In such a scenario, your silence may be misconstrued as weakness. You are then better off going on the front foot and proactively putting your point across.

The SBM had always been a subject of interest for the media. It consistently evoked strong views on both sides: the believers and the cynics. Almost everyone had an opinion on the programme, and most people's opinions were being fuelled by what they read in the papers or saw on the news. There was also a tendency for media houses and influencers who largely lived in urban areas to equate the progress of the SBM in rural areas with what they saw in urban areas. This prejudiced the views of many of them, and contributed to the general scepticism the media has about government programmes. Further, because the SBM was so closely identified with PM Modi, his detractors found the programme an effective punching bag, a means to criticize him politically.

The glass-half-empty gang

Team SBM realized very early that at the scale at which we were operating, and the level of decentralization in the implementation of the programme, there would always be some instances of gaps on the ground. For instance, there were cases of over-reporting of progress on the ground and also a few unfortunate cases of misguided field functionaries and Sarpanches coercing and intimidating people who still defecated in the open. We knew that these isolated negatives would garner a lot more attention than the overall positives, and we ensured that the state governments took strict action against the defaulters.

However, as more and more villages started declaring themselves ODF, we began to notice the overriding bias that some groups, with undoubted vested interests, had against the programme. Some of them began picking isolated instances and then painting the entire programme with a broad brush of negativity. They had developed a standard template: they would undertake field visits to two or three blocks where progress was known to be well below the national, state and district averages, find the worst villages in these already below-par regions, and try to represent these as the general truth in all of rural India. Their theory was 'If it's not working here, it cannot be working anywhere', thereby portraying the exception as the norm.

While I was the first to acknowledge that there were bound to be gaps in programme implementation, what frustrated me, especially in the early period of the job, was the refusal by some critics to even acknowledge that some good work was being done. They were not proposing any alternative theory of change either. Initially, I suffered such negativity in silence, thinking it a waste of time to respond. But then some poorly researched studies with many methodological flaws started receiving the attention of sections of the media. It became apparent to me that this was spreading misinformation and giving the public a factually incorrect representation of the SBM. And it was giving even more ammunition to those who didn't like the fact that we were making progress. This began to affect us and to divert us from our task at hand. Something had to be done.

And so, I decided to take the attack to the so-called critics by challenging their conjecture with facts, research and analytical rigour. I developed a rapid response theory: any news item that was based on conjecture rather than fact, or that made sweeping generalizations on the basis of inadequate research, would not be ignored by us at MDWS. Instead, we would respond to the publication house that carried the story with a detailed, point-by-point rebuttal on the same day, request the media house to carry our version of the story immediately, and thereby give the reader both perspectives and enable them to make an informed decision on what was true and what wasn't.

This process served two purposes. One, it helped us get our side of the story out, and that too without any major delay, while the story was still fresh in the minds of the reader. And second, it encouraged editors to exercise more stringent judgement and not let shallow and ill-researched articles pass.

If you have to explain, you've already lost the perception battle

I remember in late 2017, the United Nations Special Rapporteur on the human rights to safe drinking water and sanitation, Leo Heller, undertook an official visit to India. Mr Heller was not familiar with the SBM and took a briefing from us about the programme and the progress we had made. He then met with other stakeholders who told him what worked and what needed to be improved. Unfortunately for him, though, towards the last leg of his visit he met with some members of the glass-half-empty gang and was swayed by some of their rhetoric. At a media interaction at the end of his visit, he praised the commitment the SBM had shown to eliminate open defecation but then made a major faux pas by saying, 'Now is a critical time to replace the lens of those glasses [Gandhi's glasses] with the human rights lens.'

This obviously did not go down well with us. The Mahatma was the foremost proponent of human rights, and sanitation had been his unique and special focus. His glasses, the logo of the SBM, epitomize core human rights principles. We were shocked to learn that Mr Heller did not realize how the SBM had enhanced the quality of life and dignity of the people of rural India. In fact, this was the single biggest initiative in the world towards ensuring basic human rights. We put out our rapid response, strongly objecting to Mr Heller's observations with a point-by-point rebuttal. It was probably tough on Mr Heller, but it had to be done.

> **Pro-Tip:** Sometimes the best defence is a good offence. Go for it!

This incident reinforced my belief that once someone says something against you, some damage is already done no matter how many clarifications you offer. And so, while it was important for us to put out rejoinders against erroneous articles, I realized it was even more important to try and pre-empt them from being written in the first place.

To do this, I decided to proactively inform the misinformed. On the one hand, the communications team worked overtime to ensure that positive stories about the overall progress and field-level successes of the SBM reached the maximum number of people through all media; on the other hand, I decided to take the facts of our work to people of repute who had been thus far attacking us based on incomplete information. And so, my team and I made a list of influential persons and journalists to directly engage with and have a frank conversation about the SBM: to communicate what was going on, tell them how we were addressing any concerns they had about implementation, and listen to their suggestions on what we could do better.

While I could not win all of the media people over to our side, even the most critical of them ended up at least appreciating the effort being made at all levels. Eventually, we made our presence felt in the print media with opinion pieces written about the SBM in national newspapers by many prominent people, including politicians, civil servants, academics and celebrities. I myself wrote more than 25 op-eds in national dailies.

Trust, but verify

I also decided to request independent third parties to conduct nationally representative, large-scale surveys to verify the sanitation status of all states. These surveys not only ground-proofed our numbers, but also gave Team SBM significant leverage to be able to statistically challenge the micro surveys that some of our detractors regularly quoted.

Towards the end of 2017, an independent verification agency conducted the first round of the World Bank-funded National Annual Rural Sanitation Survey (NARSS). This was undoubtedly the most robust assessment of the sanitation status in India, supervised end to end by an empowered and Expert Working Group (EWG) co-chaired by Professor Amitabh Kundu, the eminent statistician, and Dr N.C. Saxena, the well-regarded development expert. It included statistics and sanitation specialists from the World Bank, UNICEF, BMGF, Ministry of Statistics and Programme Implementation, and other agencies. We even invited some of our regular critics to be a part of the EWG. Members also personally went to the field to check for quality control.

Two more rounds of NARSS followed in 2018–19 and 2019–20. All three found that the sanitation coverage reported by the government was more or less accurate. They also confirmed that the usage of toilets across the country was high: above 90 per cent in all three surveys. These were strong validations of the results of the SBM, and my team left no stone unturned to make these findings known to one and all through press conferences, newspaper opinion pieces and social media.

Outputs to outcomes to impact: Strengthening the narrative with research

A strong positive narrative around the SBM had already begun to develop when we began to proactively engage with global developmental agencies and request them to study the outcomes, not just in terms of toilets constructed and used, but also with respect to the positive impacts of the access to toilets on the lives of millions of people in rural India. As it turned out, the magnitude of the developmental impact of a simple toilet on the nation turned out to be much larger than I, or anyone at MDWS, had imagined.

In 2017, UNICEF carried out a study and estimated that in an ODF village, each family saved up to Rs 50,000 (about $700) per year in just medical costs they had avoided, not to mention the time savings which could be used more productively, and lives saved. Later that year, the BMGF conducted a study that found significantly lower instances of children with diarrhoea and malnourishment in ODF villages. In mid-2018, the WHO estimated that the SBM-G had saved more than 3,00,000 lives, mainly of children below the age of five, between 2014 and October 2019. In 2019, UNICEF found that ODF villages were 11.7 times less likely to have their groundwater sources contaminated. Later in the year, it estimated that the SBM had generated full-time employment for over 7.5 million people over the five-year programme period.

Such was the cross-cutting impact of the SBM-G, which contributed not just to sanitation but to improving the overall quality of life in rural India. These results were used by us in all of our established communication channels. I also personally sent out infographics on these studies to all influencers over WhatsApp, just to make sure they didn't miss it. The PMO was also frequently requested to include some of these results in the PM's speeches whenever there was an opportunity.

My team and I were always on the lookout to tell our side of the story, and tell it convincingly. All of these efforts cumulatively helped us swing the narrative in our favour. We went from being reactive to proactive, and from being defensive to being on the front foot most of the time.

Thicken your skin

I have to admit, however, that there were times when I wished I had developed a thicker skin and not been so prickly about public criticism of the SBM. In one case, after the 'Chalo Champaran' campaign in April 2018, a sarcastic tweet was put out to the effect that if 8,50,000 toilets (as Bihar state had claimed) had indeed been constructed in a week in the run-up to the 10 April Champaran event, it would mean that 84.31 toilets were constructed every minute. Now this statement obviously made no sense at all. It was not that the same set of people was constructing toilets one after the other. They were being constructed by thousands of people in hundreds of villages at the same time. However, somehow this mischievous tweet gained some traction and so we decided to respond through a press note, clarifying that the thousands of toilets had been built in tandem across the state and not sequentially. Our press note provoked another caustic tweet, so we stopped responding. In retrospect, I realized there are times when you need to take things a little lightly and either enjoy the joke or grin and bear it. It is tough to be fully objective when you are very passionate about your job, but it is an effort well worth pursuing.

Consolidating our gains for sustainability

Up until the end of 2018, our single-minded focus – almost tunnel vision – of achieving ODF status drove us towards our goal and kept us from getting distracted. By then, we had reached a sanitation coverage of over 95 per cent, and with the goal of an ODF India within striking distance, my thoughts began drifting towards the next potentially big project: piped water supply to all rural households. It was about then that I joined Indira for a few days in France, where she was representing India at the Organisation for Economic Co-operation and Development discussions on international taxation issues. When she was done with her work, we visited the famous Omaha Beach, site of one of the Normandy landings during the Second World War.

On that cold November day in Normandy, while listening to our tour guide describe the beach landing of the Allied forces on D-Day – 6 June 1944 – I had a sudden insight. I realized that even after India became ODF, there would still be unfinished business to address before venturing into something new. In any endeavour, including war, an experienced leader makes a special effort to consolidate and secure the gains made by his or her team before venturing into new territory. This is what the platoon commanders of the US Army did after finally gaining the upper hand during a fierce gun battle with the German defence forces on the beaches of Normandy on D-Day. It was critical to consolidate their hard-fought gains by securing the beachhead before venturing into German-occupied France. Similarly, I too would need to spend time and energy consolidating the gains of our ODF campaign, and institutionalizing ODF sustainability such that, with or without me, the SBM-G would ensure that people continued to use their toilets and no one defecated in the open in rural India.

Now, learning from gaps in previous sanitation programmes, we had already incorporated some quality assurance measures in the design phase itself of the SBM-G. The process followed was this: villages would declare themselves ODF, but would then be verified by a third party within three months of the declaration, and then re-verified six months from the first verification. The hypothesis was that a village that stayed ODF for about nine months would likely remain ODF for a lasting period. We found out, however, through feedback from the field, that in some isolated cases, there were 'slip backs' in the form of a few people who still defecated in the open despite having been provided with toilets. Discussions with some global behaviour change experts like Val Curtis and Cass Sunstein also made us realize that a longer engagement – of two to three years – with ODF villages was required to consolidate the ODF outcomes, sustain them and make the changed behaviour the norm.

Pro-Tip: Build an organization or a programme to last. A successful model is a sustainable one.

And so, we decided on a three-pronged strategy: to renew the Darwaza Band mass media campaign with a sustainability focus and the tagline 'Har koi, har roz, hamesha' (Everybody, every day, always); to launch a massive capacity-strengthening campaign of all swachhagrahis and grassroots-level elected officials; and to launch a campaign termed 'No One Left Behind' to provide toilets to new households that would join in the future.

Fast-forward to a few months later. With the country's five-yearly national elections just a few months away, it was time to articulate our vision of the future of sanitation in rural India, in order to present our strategic road map to the new government soon after it took office. At the core of the vision was the concept of an ODF Plus village – one that sustained ODF behaviour and also safely managed its solid and liquid waste. This formed the basis for the creation of a 10-Year Sanitation Strategy document in my penultimate year at the Ministry.

Renewing the drinking water agenda

You may remember that rural drinking water was also a part of my portfolio. And while I initially focused more on the SBM, my water team and I did introduce some significant reforms in the ongoing National Rural Drinking Water Programme. Our funding to states became much more performance-oriented and scheme-specific, in a departure from the inefficient, unconditional grant-giving system of the past. We also introduced an element of competition, à la SBM, encouraging the states to deliver on their agreed targets before being granted additional funds from a fixed pot of central funds.

These reforms, quite significant at the time, came about as a result of frequent interaction with Nripendra Mishra and his team at the PMO, and were formally approved by the Union Cabinet in November 2017. One of the most experienced officers in the Government of India, Mr Mishra brought all his acumen to bear on the matter as we engaged in a dialogue on reforming the rural drinking water sector.

The case for a national drinking water programme

In discussions with the PMO about a new national rural drinking water programme, I proposed that in areas where sufficient and clean groundwater was available, each village should implement their own small groundwater-based piped water supply scheme. Larger water supply schemes transporting water from rivers or reservoirs to many villages should only be implemented in groundwater-stressed areas or areas affected by water quality issues. Additionally, interventions to sustain the source of water, such as groundwater recharge, rainwater harvesting, and reuse of treated household wastewater, would be mandatory for all schemes, big or small. States would be financially incentivized based on a combination of performance and requirement, with a higher weightage to states with meagre water resources. The funds would be pooled in from different central and state schemes through convergence. And of course, as our experience from the SBM taught us, when the PM prioritized a programme and a dedicated team got to work to realize his vision, results followed.

The fruits of labour are sweet

Arguably, two of the most surreal moments of my life as Secretary to the Government of India came within 45 days of each other. The first was on 15 August 2019, when the PM announced the Jal Jeevan Mission (JJM; the evocative name he gave to the new national rural drinking water programme) from the Red Fort. It brought back memories of his speech exactly five years ago, when, in Vietnam, Indira and I had watched him on TV promising the nation the 'impossible dream' of the SBM. Now, five years later, Indira and I were sitting together again, this time in the Red Fort, only a few yards away from the PM, on the brink of achieving the SBM dream and primed to hear him announce another mega flagship programme: drinking water for all through the JJM. It was an unforgettable moment for both of us.

And just as at the time of the SBM, over the next few months, we had a new team for water, led by the new and very capable Additional Secretary, Bharat Lal, who came with plenty of experience in designing and managing rural drinking water programmes in Gujarat.

The next, and possibly the most surreal, moment came soon after, on 2 October 2019, the 150th birth anniversary of Mahatma Gandhi, the day the PM had spoken about repeatedly for five years: the day the Swachh Bharat Mission achieved the unthinkable. I have to say it was an incredibly emotional moment for me and my entire team when the PM announced at a grand evening ceremony that India had declared itself ODF – just as he had promised the nation five years ago. The event, at which the PM dedicated a Swachh Bharat to Mahatma Gandhi, took place on the banks of the Sabarmati river in Ahmedabad, close to Gandhiji's Sabarmati Ashram. Indira was in the audience too, along with over 20,000 swachhagrahis watching the PM laud their efforts over the past five years. He spoke about how this was not the end of the journey, but a major milestone, and that there was a long road ahead for achieving a truly Swachh Bharat. He also spoke about the path to achieving household piped connections for all rural households through the new JJM. I still have fond recollections of that memorable evening in Ahmedabad.

16

Expect the unexpected

… AND ALONG CAME THE CORONAVIRUS

IF THERE IS one thing I have learned over my long career, it is that one can never predict what will happen next and that, in Robert Burns' words, 'The best laid schemes o' mice an' men / Gang aft a-gley' (go awry). Something unexpected will come up when you least expect it, but I don't think the word 'unexpected' even begins to describe the arrival of the coronavirus pandemic in India in March 2020.

In the weeks immediately after 2 October 2019, there was a feeling of an anti-climax. The journey until that point had been a roller-coaster ride, with a thrill a minute. The work had been action-packed and each day had felt like a mini mission in itself, with the drive to achieve the PM's goal keeping us going full throttle. Knowing we had achieved what we had set out to do was very satisfying, but my feeling that it was now time to hand over the reins to someone else, and move on, deepened. I spent the next few months with the Department of Drinking Water and Sanitation* (DDWS) team in carefully planning for Phase-II of the SBM, as well as for the implementation of the new drinking water programme, the JJM. (The Ministry of Water Resources, River Development and Ganga Rejuvenation and the Ministry of Drinking Water and Sanitation were merged to create a new Ministry of Jal Shakti in May 2019, with the DDWS now part of it.)

The COVID-19 googly

Around this time, Indira, also immersed in her work at the Tax Policy Research Unit, Ministry of Finance, and I had started thinking about a life outside government, back in the US with Tara and Venkat. We both felt that the coming period should be focused on family.

Meanwhile, I continued to make field trips and made a hectic visit to Bihar during 13–15 March where, accompanied by my team, we covered 15 districts in three days, meeting DMs and SBM beneficiaries, and discussing JJM implementation issues with local officials. We garnered a tremendous response from the DMs, so much so that I decided to return to Bihar the following week, much to the chagrin of our state counterparts who anticipated more 17-hour workdays coming up. But by then, the COVID-19 pandemic had taken over, the number of positive cases in India was rising, and it did not make sense to travel. I called off the trip. To reduce the risk of transmission of the coronavirus, I encouraged most of the office staff to work from home. Only a week later, on 24 March, the PM announced a nationwide lockdown.

---

*   By this time, the MDWS had become a Department under the newly formed Ministry of Jal Shakti.

We had our own little pre-lockdown drama at home during this period. Indira had left for the US in early March to spend some time there with Tara and Venkat. In mid-March, many countries around the world had started imposing travel restrictions on air travel, stopping both inbound and outbound flights. Indira was scheduled to return to Delhi on 17 March but decided to postpone her return by a few days. In the meantime, the Indian government took a sudden decision to stop all incoming flights into the country starting midnight of 21 March. Luckily for us, Indira's Air India flight from Washington to Delhi was scheduled to land at noon on 21 March. Her flight was delayed by a few hours, but she managed to make it back and home-quarantined herself for the required 14 days.

The new normal

It was a bizarre experience – the entire COVID-19 situation. On one hand, there was a raging pandemic to worry about. On the other, the government had to carry out its business despite the restrictions. In my line of work, not only were we at a crucial stage of the SBM, with the recent launch of Phase-II of the programme, but early into the lockdown, I was called to the PMO and informed about the constitution of Empowered Groups to deal with various aspects of the lockdown situation. I was made the convenor of Empowered Group No. 5 (EG5): facilitating logistics and supply chain management of essential items like food and medicines.

Adapting quickly to the changed circumstances, my entire DDWS team and I began to work from home and connected with each other via technology. To my relief, all of us adapted to this 'new normal' working environment soon. We scheduled regular review meetings, brainstorming sessions and catch-up discussions via videoconferencing, and I soon found this was an efficient way of doing business. This way, we were able to stay on the topic of discussion without much deviation and could get a lot of work done in a relatively short time. A week into the lockdown, I actually began enjoying the new 'virtual' experience.

> **Pro-Tip:** There will often be equally important tasks which need to be delivered in parallel. Learn to walk and chew gum at the same time.

Indira and I were also experiencing a 'new normal' at home. It was back to our Washington DC days where, without any domestic help, we had to do all the housework ourselves. To be honest, 90 per cent of the work in DC, cooking, cleaning etc., had been done by Indira, on top of her office work. With the excuse of my frequent travel, the most I had done was occasionally take care of the vacuuming and lawn mowing and cook the rare dal-sabzi. Now, as before, she handled most of the housework with aplomb, cleaning the house and cooking meals, but this time I played a more significant role, helping to wash the clothes, iron some of them and even sometimes cook a more elaborate dish. I must mention that the already multi-skilled Indira acquired another new skill during this period: haircutting! With all nearby barbershops shut down, she volunteered to trim my now very unkempt hair, and did a pretty good job of it.

During the lockdown period, both Indira and I intensified our physical fitness routines. I got up even earlier in the morning, now at 4.30 a.m., and did a 5 km run on the treadmill, then lifted some weights in our little home gym, and ended with a few pull-ups on a bar in the garden. Since all outdoor activities, including travel and golf, had stopped, this was the perfect opportunity to start writing this book and I managed to log in two or three hours of daily writing at the crack of dawn.

The new 'mission': Managing the national supply chain of food and medicines

The Empowered Group of which I was made convener had 12 members, all senior officers from other Ministries, including some Secretaries to the Government of India. We were given the mandate to come up with solutions to ease the supply chain bottlenecks for essential items and report directly to the PMO.

This was a major responsibility. One of the biggest fears many business leaders and economists had when the lockdown was announced was the total disruption of logistics and the supply chain, especially of essential items. If people were not allowed to move around and go to their production units and workplace, they wouldn't be able to produce essential items. Transporters wouldn't be able to transport these items across states. Warehouses wouldn't be able to function. Exports and imports would stop and ports would get jammed. The entire logistics machinery would come to a grinding halt!

While I had no formal training in logistics and supply chain management, my experience as DM in Bijnor, handling the post-Ayodhya law and order situation, plus all the field experience and crisis management skills I had acquired over my IAS career came in very handy. I also relished this unique opportunity on two counts: one, it was a nationally important task and would significantly contribute to ensuring that people across the country continued to have access to essential items during the lockdown, and two, it brought back some of the high adrenaline action I had begun to miss after 2 October 2019. I wasted no time. Apart from working closely with the Ministries dealing with transport and essential supplies, I also reached out to some logistics and supply chain experts for advice on how we could begin to define the challenges in the current situation and identify structural solutions. Additionally, we also set up mechanisms to collect and analyse data, coordinated with industry associations, designed progress indicators, identified bottlenecks and worked with states almost on a daily basis to troubleshoot specific instances of supply chain breakdowns.

The first Monday after the lockdown began and I was back in office, this time wearing a mask. My colleagues Samir, Yugal, Vineet and Gosain of course were with me, all masked up as well. We also had two new teams of subject matter experts working with us pro bono. And I invited V. Radha, my former JS, who was on childcare leave, to join this effort if she could, and she gladly agreed. I must admit it was rather surreal that first day, with everyone sitting far apart in my large office, wearing masks and being virtually unrecognizable. We had sanitizer dispensers mounted every 10 m on the walls. Our customary coffee during meetings was probably the only thing that was just the same as before, as we violated the 'keep the mask on' rule to get our caffeine fix in.

Later in the day, we had our very first videoconference with the rest of the members of EG5, followed by meetings with Resident Commissioners of all states, national associations of truckers, associations of FMCG companies, e-commerce players, dairy producers, vegetable mandis and a host of supply chain and logistics experts. Those first couple of days were a steep learning curve on the jargon and the nuances of the logistics and supply chain world for my team and me.

Donning many different hats

The first hat I donned for this new undertaking was that of a process consultant. Through all the information we gathered, we identified the structural gaps in the process and, within a few days, we made representations to the Ministry of Home Affairs for certain relaxations. We proposed to allow the free movement of trucks with one driver and one helper across the country without a pass but with the driver producing his driving licence, whether the truck was carrying essential or non-essential goods. This was important as truck drivers across the country were being stopped at interstate borders and even at district borders with the local police taking suo moto decisions on what was essential and what wasn't. This had led to the number of trucks on the road dropping from about 2 million per day pre-lockdown to under 2,00,000 per day, severely crippling national supply chains.

The second hat I donned was that of a perpetual troubleshooter. We collected information from many sources on where supply chains were broken. I would then call up Chief Secretaries and, in many cases, DMs to 'de-bottleneck' them. It helped that I was among the most senior civil servants in the government, and so everyone I called was either happy to solve problems for me or just did it to address my 'nuisance value'! Often, to my amusement, when I called a DM, they would, before I could say anything, immediately start telling me that they planned to start ODF Plus activities as soon as the lockdown ended, only to be relieved to learn that I was calling them for something other than the SBM this time. They would always follow my orders immediately and I almost felt like I was a DM again.

The third, and probably the most unexpected, hat I donned was that of an auctioneer in a vegetable mandi. Well, not literally. A few weeks into the lockdown we had developed a sophisticated data management system and dashboard. And then we decided to go one step further. We knew there were many places with surplus supplies of fruits and vegetables, and many others which had a shortage. But this demand and supply were not able to speak to each other at the marketplace because most of them were shut down. And so, my team and I organized a videoconference connecting the sellers – state governments representing their farmers with surplus produce – directly with the buyers – the biggest wholesalers and e-commerce traders in the country. I played the role of the facilitator, middleman and even the 'auctioneer'.

Meanwhile, in Swachh Bharat…

Alongside the work of EG5, Swachh Bharat was moving well into its second phase and the state machineries were motivated to get their acts in order as the new fight for achieving ODF Plus villages ensued. In Delhi, my team and I were working furiously to complete the construction and development of the *Rashtriya Swachhata Kendra* (National Sanitation Centre, RSK for short) a high-tech experience centre at Rajghat in New Delhi. A tribute to Mahatma Gandhi, the RSK was first announced by the PM on 10 April 2017 at the completion of 100 years of the Champaran Satyagraha. Now that an ODF India had been achieved, it was time to develop what we hoped would be a magnificently curated high-tech centre that did not just tell the tale of how the ODF battle was won, but was also a one-stop shop for children to dive into the spirit of the *jan andolan* in an edutainment format.

There were many twists and turns in the process of creating the RSK. In March 2020, before the onset of the pandemic in India, I had approached the PMO to request that the PM consider inaugurating the RSK on 10 April 2020, exactly three years from when he announced it in 2017. He said yes but the lockdown came in the way and we had to postpone the inauguration, which was not such a bad thing, since it gave us a little more time to complete the task in the best possible way. Things got so delayed that I had to step in, this time wearing the hat of a contractor, and use my EG5 contacts in the railways to arrange for some scarce 'ready-mix concrete' (in short supply due to the lockdown) from a railway construction site for the construction of the arched entrance gate of the RSK. Waving more of the stick than the carrot, I must confess, to deal with the innumerable excuses of the actual contractor for the delay in project completion, we finally managed to get the RSK ready just in time for its inauguration by PM Modi on 8 August 2020 (Quit India Day). This was my tenth and final event with the PM and, from an optics point of view, the most surreal. We were all masked up throughout his visit due to the ongoing pandemic.

Back to some good old behaviour change

Amidst all the frantic activity involving the RSK and the supply chain, safe sanitation and good hygiene practices remained the backbone of the pandemic world over. With no cure in sight and a vaccine at least a year away, the first line of defence remained prevention, with its roots firmly settled in sanitation and hygiene: physical distancing, wearing masks, not spitting in public places, handwashing with soap, and of course using a toilet. It was at this time that my fumble with Amitabh Bachchan occurred – which had to do with fuelling panic about 'virus spreading flies'.

Happy that Mr Bachchan has not blocked my number yet

My association with Mr Bachchan, again courtesy my friendship with the former Commissioner of Police, Mumbai, had been somewhat of a comedy of errors. While his engagement with the SBM as our most famous ambassador remained constant, I did manage to trip a few times when it came to engaging with him. In fact, I did so the very first time I ever emailed him, after our first meeting in Mumbai – when, like any other diehard Bachchan fan, I was star-struck. I still cringe about his response when I recall it: he wrote that I had got the spelling of his last name wrong!

My most recent fumble with Mr Bachchan came during the lockdown period. *The Lancet* had published a paper, based on a study done on COVID-19 patients in China, which concluded that the coronavirus had a much longer shelf life when contained in human faeces, as opposed to surviving in respiratory samples. In fact, the study said that in some samples the virus had remained active for almost five weeks more than in the respiratory samples. We, Team SBM, thought we had a smoking gun to present to the people on why using one's toilet, as opposed to defecating in the open, was now more important than ever. We approached Mr Bachchan and, true to his word, within 24 hours he sent us a video message in the form of a public service announcement. We went to town with it! We requested him to share it over social media with his 40 million followers, and he did. We sent it to all major media channels to carry, and they did.

The call from my good friend Preeti Sudan, Secretary in the Ministry of Health, which was leading the fight against

COVID-19, came just a few hours after the news channels had begun carrying the message. What we hadn't counted on was the panic we would cause. Each message was followed by TV anchors exclaiming that now even flies could carry the coronavirus! In a country where a nationwide lockdown was in place and people were already fearful of the unknown virus, we had gone ahead and shaken everyone with the message that now, thanks to excreta-carrying flies, they were not even safe at home. The Ministry of Health spokesperson made a categorical statement that COVID-19 was not a vector-borne disease and could not be transmitted through flies.

To cut a long story short, we withdrew the message across all media platforms, and I had the unfortunate task of calling Mr Bachchan to give him the damaging news and to request him to delete his Twitter post. I am very fortunate that Mr Bachchan is as kind as he is humble, for he did not once let on that he was upset or disappointed but simply did as I requested. Within a week, he had already agreed to do another public service announcement for us on the supply chain and logistics warriors during the national lockdown. I cannot express my gratitude enough to Amitabhji, who has always put the nation first.

'Unparliamentary' jokes

The fumble with Mr Bachchan was a minor setback, but we took it in stride. As June 2020 approached, amidst the still rising number of active cases of the coronavirus, the restrictions employed under the national lockdown were being relaxed. This meant that the new normal was going to bring people out of isolation and back to workplaces, even as they adopted all necessary safety precautions and personal hygiene practices. We immediately jumped at the opportunity and designed a behaviour change campaign based on two important themes: *lives* and *livelihood*. The former focused on health- and hygiene-related behaviours for individuals to adopt in their day-to-day activities, while the latter focused on curbing panic and encouraging people to get back to work, assured of government assistance and armed with safety precautions.

The highlight of the campaign was a special short film, to be done by none other than our favourite ambassador, Akshay Kumar. Akshay, ever ready to jump in, immediately agreed when I called him with the proposition and even brought filmmaker R. Balki to help with producing the spot.

It took a bit of back and forth to get this film done, given the situation. We had lockdowns delaying the process, and with all our creative juices flowing, the script went through rapid changes. Anyhow, we finally hit D-Day and I remember receiving a call from Akshay while he was on his way to the shoot at a film studio in coronavirus-infested Mumbai. He said, 'Mr Iyer, I must tell you, my wife is very annoyed with you right now.'

The film was a conversation between Bablu (Akshay) and a village Sarpanch, where they discuss the precautions everyone should take to be able to safely return to work. It was a smooth film, except at the end, where the Sarpanch wears his mask incorrectly, not covering his nose properly. Bablu corrects him, saying, '*Arre Sarpanchji, kachhe bhi kya aise pehente ho? Naak toh dhak lo!*' (Oh Sarpanch, do you also wear your underwear like this? Cover your nose please!) Thankfully, I caught this 'unparliamentary' joke and, much to Akshay's and Balki's disappointment, had it removed.

Bringing down the curtain

When the fourth extension of the lockdown ended in June 2020, the logistics and supply chain of essential items had more or less been restored and we were almost back to a steady state. I met the PM in July and requested to be relieved of my duties. He was very understanding and agreed with my request. It was time for Indira and me to return to the US and rejoin Tara and Venkat.

As we packed up our lives once again, Indira and I witnessed our last Independence Day speech at the Red Fort on 15 August 2020 – all masked up and appropriately socially distanced. The success of the SBM figured in the PM's speech this time, along with a progress report on the first year of JJM implementation. Five days later, Indira and I had a private farewell meeting with the PM, where he was kind enough to appreciate the work done over the past four and a half years.

Time had indeed flown since the day I joined the IAS as a callow probationer at the Lal Bahadur Shastri National Academy of Administration in Mussoorie. Looking back, I had to almost pinch myself to believe I had actually undergone such an incredible insider–outsider–insider journey – from the early 'insider' years in UP and Delhi, to the 'outsider' years in the World Bank in Washington DC coupled with my unforgettable road manager stint, followed by my second 'insider' stint in the Government of India, where I became the longest serving Secretary in recent times. How lucky could one get to have had such a varied career.

Fortunately, with all the hustle and bustle and hectic activity of winding up our house establishment at the New Moti Bagh Colony, I didn't have too much time to wax sentimental about leaving the best job of my life. There were no elaborate farewells in COVID times, and Indira and I bade quiet goodbyes to our friends and office colleagues. On 23 August, we flew out on the non-stop Air India flight to Washington DC. I was an outsider again.

Pro-Tip: Leave when people say 'why?', not 'why not?'.

Post Script

THERE WAS AN overwhelming sense of déjà vu when I returned to the World Bank in Washington DC in August 2020. Like the last time when I rejoined, I am now back at the same career level as when I left the World Bank in early 2016. The job this time is to promote and scale up sanitation and hygiene in the World Bank's client countries across the world – even more important now in the context of the ongoing coronavirus pandemic. I miss the relentless pressure and day-to-day excitement of my long stint as Secretary to the Government of India, but have begun enjoying my new work and its intercontinental spread. I am, in a sense, back to being a travelling salesman, travelling (virtually, until the COVID-19 restrictions are lifted) to different countries instead of Indian states, and sprinkling around *gyan* (wisdom).

It was great for Indira and me to catch up with Tara and Venkat. Tara is now an economist with the International Monetary Fund and Venkat the Director of Business Development at his old tennis academy near College Park, Maryland. Indira had resigned from her position in the Ministry of Finance,

Government of India, and is now planning to take up consulting on economic and fiscal issues. We have leased an apartment in Bethesda, Maryland, near our own rambling house, currently still on rent, and are looking forward to returning to the latter in a few months. Fortified by my recent refresher on housework during the Delhi lockdown, I am attempting to do some cooking at home and vacuuming the house on weekends. The competitive spirit still burns in me, however, as I battle with Venkat on the golf course during weekends.

The frenetic tempo of life in Delhi has now settled down to a steady beat in Washington DC. There is undoubtedly more method in my life now than madness and, while I sometimes miss the latter, I have started enjoying the relatively anonymous life and being away from the spotlight.

Instead of my old routine of the early-morning drive from Bethesda to Washington DC, the coffee and 'everything' bagel at the Starbucks on Pennsylvania Avenue, and the short walk to my office, I now go for an early-morning run and end up at the local Bethesda Starbucks. Checking my emails while sipping coffee outdoors, I still enjoy catching up with the news from Indian friends and former colleagues. Sometimes, however, a part of me yearns to return to the action in Delhi. Who knows, one day I might get another fateful call – and become an insider again!

Washington DC   **Parameswaran Iyer**
December 2020

Index

About the Author

PARAMESWARAN IYER is currently the Global Lead for Strategic Initiatives in the World Bank's Water Global Practice. Prior to this, he served as Secretary to the Government of India at the Ministry of Drinking Water and Sanitation (later, Department of Drinking Water and Sanitation under the newly formed Ministry of Jal Shakti), from March 2016 until August 2020, and led the implementation of the flagship Swachh Bharat Mission. A former IAS officer, Iyer headed the innovative community-led Swajal Project in Uttar Pradesh and Uttarakhand in the 1990s, has over twenty-five years of global experience in the water and sanitation sector and has worked in many countries, including Vietnam, China, Egypt and Lebanon. A fitness enthusiast, Iyer also served as road manager to his daughter and son on the pro tennis circuit during a two-year sabbatical from his professional career.